MATT MORAN

Matt Moran is head chef and co-owner of ARIA restaurant, which is enviably located at the doorstep of the Sydney Opera House, and overlooks the harbour. Matt's established reputation has taken him to all corners of the world, landing him invitations to cook in such places as New York's esteemed James Beard Foundation, and to act as culinary consultant to Singapore Airlines. He has also featured in the television series *My Restaurant Rules* and *Heat in the Kitchen*.

MATT MORAN

with photography by Geoff Lung

LANTERN
an imprint of
PENGUIN BOOKS

Dedicated to Amelia Alice and Harry Hopkins

Contents

Foreword

Matt Moran and I have been friends for over fifteen years. He is, quite simply, an inspired chef. He believes in using the best of seasonal ingredients (a credo close to my heart) and creating dishes where each ingredient complements the others with absolutely no false notes. It is always fascinating for me to see how he has created an intensely personal signature food style by distilling the flavours of the global cuisines available to Australia and adding all kinds of wonderful, confident touches of his own. It is obvious that for Matt cooking is sheer joy and, though this is perhaps a strange word to use when speaking of cooking, I admire the integrity of his food.

Matt's career has been quite extraordinary and will be an inspiration to any young chef just starting out. Matt's enthusiasm shows in every page of this fantastic book – a repertoire of delicious recipes which I am sure will motivate dedicated home cooks and professional chefs around the world. Just keep in mind that this enthusiasm is contagious. Once you have read this book and tried some of the recipes, your own style of cooking will be permanently influenced by Matt's lively combinations and his renowned light touch. And personally, I think that is a good thing!

Gordon Ramsay

Introduction

Growing up on a dairy farm in Badgerys Creek, on the western fringes of Sydney, I drank milk like other kids drink water. One of my most vivid early memories is of walking through the old stone dairy on the way to school as the milk truck arrived. My brother and I would wait while the milk was drained from the enormous steel vat. There was always some left in the pipe and we'd pull our cups out of our schoolbags and take what was left. Fresh, icy-cold milk. I can still taste it.

Apart from that, I had what is probably a pretty typical Australian upbringing when it came to food: meat and three vegetables, no sight of fish – I'm pretty sure my first restaurant meal was at a Black Stump steakhouse when I was fourteen. Without ever having tasted it, I was convinced I hated seafood. I think I can honestly say the only food I had any kind of passion for was that milk straight from the vat and my Nan Valda's date scones (at 93, she still makes the best scones I've ever tasted!).

I can probably also thank my rural upbringing for instilling in me a work ethic and a certain toughness. As a kid, any spare time I had was spent helping out around the farm. At a young age, my brother and I were given a lot of responsibility. Dad would send us off in the tractor to feed the cattle. We'd point it down the hill in low gear, jumping down at intervals to throw off the hay. I remember one day we didn't realise how far we'd gone and the tractor ploughed straight over the fence; luckily, I always had my older brother to take the blame! The work was hard, but it was a lot of fun.

When I was nine we hit hard times on the farm and moved to Seven Hills, in Sydney's western suburbs. Even then, Dad managed to buy a smaller farm at Taralga, in the Southern Tablelands, and every weekend we went to crutch and drench and mark the sheep. We slaughtered our own meat and at that early age I developed an interest in butchery, and a real passion for farming. Now we have a 2000-acre property at Rockley, beyond the Blue Mountains, about three hours' drive west of Sydney, farming fat lambs and cattle. Nothing gives me greater joy than spending time there with my family, watching my four-year-old son, Harry, sitting on my dad's knee while he's driving the tractor, or taking him to gather the eggs in the chook pen and then cooking them up for breakfast.

Living in Seven Hills, I went to school in the Blacktown area, and the best thing I can say about the experience is that my desperation to leave drove me to an early start in my career as a chef. A typical class would involve a kid throwing some kind of missile – an orange or a pencil-case – at the teacher, causing the teacher to storm out and the rest of us to be left to amuse ourselves for whatever time remained. The kids wouldn't listen, and the teachers gave up. I remember my science teacher pulling me up once to tell me I was a loser and that I'd never amount to anything in life. As an uncertain teenager, I wasn't sure whether or not I should believe him.

It was about that time a friend and I decided to take Home Science. The classes were in the afternoon and we knew we'd get a feed . . . We'd also get to spend the hour with the eighteen girls who took Home Science. For the exam I made a banana split: grilled banana with ice cream and chocolate sauce. It was the first thing I remember cooking. And it was bloody awful.

So, people ask me all the time what got me into cooking. I'd like to say a passion for food. But the truth is I hated school and needed a way out. I split my year-ten work experience between the bakery at Woolworths in Blacktown and a butcher's shop in Cabramatta. Armed with minimal skills, I left school and worked over the summer in the kitchen at the Parramatta RSL. When the grill chef got an order for meat, I was the lackey who ran to the cool room to get it. I remember watching in awe as the chef broke an egg in one hand, and thinking to myself if I could do that, I'd make a great chef. The RSL offered me an apprenticeship to start in July, but my dad wouldn't let me hang around doing nothing until then, so I had to go back to school. Every free minute I had was spent looking for another job, phone call after phone call, one interview to the next. Dad drove me to every interview and waited in the car. Then one day in March 1985 I saw an ad for a first-year apprentice at a restaurant in Roseville, on Sydney's upper North Shore, called La Belle Helene. I remember saying to Dad that there wasn't any point in going to the interview – it was an hour and a half on the train and I felt I didn't stand a chance. But he just said I'd made the appointment and bundled me into the car. I even borrowed his leather jacket to look half decent. Looking back, it turned out to be one of the most important days of my life.

I knew nothing about the restaurant, but it was probably the best on the North Shore at the time. Sitting across the table from me in the dining room was Michael De Laurence, the man who would be my head chef and mentor for the next four years. When I saw a list of names in front of him, with ticks or crosses next to them, I knew that to get this job I'd need to lay it on the line. I came straight out with it and said: 'If you give me this job, you will not be sorry. Just give me a go.' Not much else was said. He told me to come in and do a three-day trial. Arriving on day one, my plan was to keep my mouth shut and do what I was told. So I did. The first thing he asked me to do was to strain the game stock. At the RSL all our sauces had come in tubs. I didn't have a clue what stock was. So I strained the stock down the sink and duly took the bones out to Michael. He told me to throw them out. *But if I throw out the bones,* I thought, blood draining from my face, *I'll have nothing left.* Needless to say when I came clean with Michael, the proverbial hit the fan. Two nights later I was stunned when he told me I could go to school on Monday and tell them I was leaving. But I did exactly that. I went to every single one of my teachers and told them that I wouldn't be coming back.

At La Belle we worked six days a week, up to fifteen hours a day. Michael ran an incredibly tight ship. There were days I thought I would've been better off in the army, but the fact was, as a fifteen-year-old kid from Blacktown, I had a lot to learn about discipline. I remember the sous-chef telling me to wipe my bench clean when I thought it was already spotless, and kicking me on the back of the legs when I wasn't standing with even pressure on both feet. At first I hated her with her with every breath of my being, but within months I worked out she was doing the hard yards with me, and I gratefully fell under her wing.

Every night when Dad picked me up, the question would be the same: 'Are you sure this is what you want to do?' He was worried that if I dropped out of my apprenticeship I wouldn't be able to get back into school. It didn't matter how many times I told him I was enjoying it. In fact, even though I'd stumbled into it, after the first couple of days it was a love affair. Coming from such a simple food background, to see what could be done with food was a revelation to me. Each day I couldn't wait to get to work, to learn new things, acquire new skills. Every time the menu changed, I was like a kid in a candy store. I pretty much spent every waking hour of my teenage years in the kitchen of La Belle Helene, and I don't regret a minute of it. I even started a small business on the side: I made a batch of tarts – winter fruit, mandarin, date – and approached a couple of the local delis. Pretty soon I was making between thirty and forty a week. I'd finish work at midnight, bake until two or three in the morning and then get up at seven to finish them off.

Before I had finished my apprenticeship at La Belle, I was sous-chef, and in my last six months there, Michael concentrated on a new venture and left me to run the kitchen. When he returned, I realised it was time for me to move on. Handing my resignation to Michael was one of the hardest things I've had to do. It felt like leaving home.

Soon after, in 1990, I spoke with Stefano Manfredi, and he offered me a job as sous-chef at the Restaurant Manfredi in Ultimo, which was then widely regarded as the best Italian restaurant in the country. After cooking French food for nearly five years, it was an opportunity I couldn't turn down. During the two years there, Stefano and Franca taught me a lot about the simplicity of a good menu and the importance of quality produce. After work I'd often meet up with my mate Peter Sullivan for a drink and we'd concoct plans to open our own restaurant. I'd got to know Peter at La Belle Helene, where he'd been a waiter and later the restaurant manager. He had a real passion for the industry, and I just knew he would make a great business partner. In October 1991, when the opportunity arose to take over the bistro at the Paddington Inn, in Sydney's eastern suburbs, Peter and I jumped at it. After a month of trading I remember sitting with Peter and thinking how good it was that we had so much money in the bank; what we didn't think about was that we hadn't yet paid any of our suppliers! Paddington Inn was a steep learning curve for us, as we discovered that running a restaurant entailed so much more than just cooking and looking after customers. Pete and I ran on adrenaline. We'd start at the fruit and veg markets at 4 a.m., work all day, finish at midnight, then play pool until dawn. After three years of hard work we were delighted to receive a coveted 'Chef's Hat' in the *Sydney Morning Herald Good Food Guide*.

Moving to bistro food from the fine-dining kitchens of La Belle Helene and Restaurant Manfredi was a fun challenge for me. I really warmed to the concept of comfort food: simple, rustic, and most of all delicious. I think of it as food to nourish the soul – some of my favourite comfort-food recipes are Taglierini with Green Vegetables and Butter, Duck and Pea Pie with Pea Purée and Quince Clafoutis, all of which I regularly cook at home. I hope you enjoy making and eating them as much as I do.

After 3½ years running the Paddington Inn Bistro, in 1995 Pete and I saw the old Merivale building in Potts Point come up for lease, and thought it would be a great place for our next move – a wonderful space in a great inner-city neighbourhood. We could divide the space into two areas: a simple café and a fine-dining restaurant. For me, it was the best of both worlds. Morans won the 'Best New Restaurant' award in the 1996 *Good Food Guide* and, in its third year of operation, went from one to two Chef's Hats. During that time Pete and I also branched out and opened another restaurant, Bonne Femme, in East Sydney, with our sous-chef of many years, Genevieve Copeland, at the helm.

In 1999 we were asked if we'd be interested in a space in a new and highly controversial building at Circular Quay, dubbed 'The Toaster'. The picketing against the development, protesting its encroachment on the Opera House precinct, hadn't long stopped, and our initial reaction was not to go anywhere near it. But one day we were persuaded to go and have a look: from the moment I saw it, I just knew that this would be our new restaurant's home. Such an amazing space and position, and how could I resist the opportunity to build my own kitchen from scratch? With the sparkling waters of Sydney Harbour and the Opera House almost close enough to touch, the name ARIA seemed true to our vision of a timeless restaurant. When it came to the design, we enlisted the remarkable talents of Alex Tzannes and Jonathan Evans, who envisaged ARIA's interior as the inside of a classic old Mercedes Benz, simple and elegant. The restaurant opened in December 1999, ten days before the start of the new millennium, and we haven't looked back since.

As the business grew, and ARIA's reputation spread both locally and internationally, we were able to attract staff from all over the world – I now have a kitchen brigade with chefs from Japan, the UK and the rest of Europe working alongside my local chefs and apprentices. These guys bring a wealth of information and skills to both me and my kitchen. I still spend many hours each week cooking in the kitchen, and I still love it as much as I did the day I started.

For me personally, ARIA has been the launching pad for some fantastic opportunities, such as cooking at the James Beard Foundation in New York and making my first television appearances as a judge on *My Restaurant Rules* and in the behind-the-scenes documentary *Heat in the Kitchen*. In 2003 I was also invited to be part of the International Culinary Panel for Singapore Airlines, along with chefs such as Gordon Ramsay, Alfred Portale and Georges Blanc. To work with those guys and discuss global directions in food is a great privilege – not to mention handy for securing restaurant bookings in their home cities! I now travel more often and relish the opportunity to eat in some of the best restaurants in the world.

What has been a real joy to me over the last few years is seeing some of our local produce improving so much in quality that it matches or even surpasses its overseas counterparts. Our wagyu beef is but one example.

In the twenty years that I've been cooking, Australian produce has gone from strength to strength. When I started out, most of the crustaceans were frozen, there was no grain-fed meat or poultry, and the only zucchini flowers came from domestic vegetable gardens. Pork was typically lean and dry – there was none of the juicy, old-fashioned pork now marketed as Kurobuta or Bangalow. Nor was there a thriving aquaculture industry producing such delicacies as Hiramasa kingfish, Spring Bay mussels and Suzuki jewfish. With amazing new products every year, it is just so exciting to be a chef now.

One of the most enjoyable aspects of my work is sharing my enthusiasm for food, whether it be through cooking classes or my chef's tours. I love to take people to the markets and watch them get as excited as I do about great produce, and then bring it all back to have some fun with it in the ARIA kitchen. Witnessing the public's growing fascination with food has led us to open a chef's

table at ARIA, with an unobstructed view of the kitchen, so diners can see for themselves the workings of a busy kitchen (and occasionally watch as a chef loses the plot . . .).

And now I want to share my recipes with you. This book has been a long time coming. In it you will find recipes and dishes developed over my twenty years of cooking. Some of them are more challenging than others: recipes such as Peking Duck Consommé or Poached Lamb Loin with Basil Mousse and Lentils may appear daunting, but most of the more difficult recipes can be broken down into smaller components. I encourage you simply to work through the recipes, step by step. My strong belief is that good produce should be allowed to speak for itself. We cook to enhance and highlight flavour – and, remember, we cook for enjoyment.

People always say to me, 'I bet you don't cook at home.' But the truth is, it is probably my favourite place to cook. At home, I can let the mood take me, which means that I get as much pleasure from cooking Croque Monsieur for a family brunch as I do from spending hours over a classic Cassoulet for a big dinner party. I hope this book enables you to do the same.

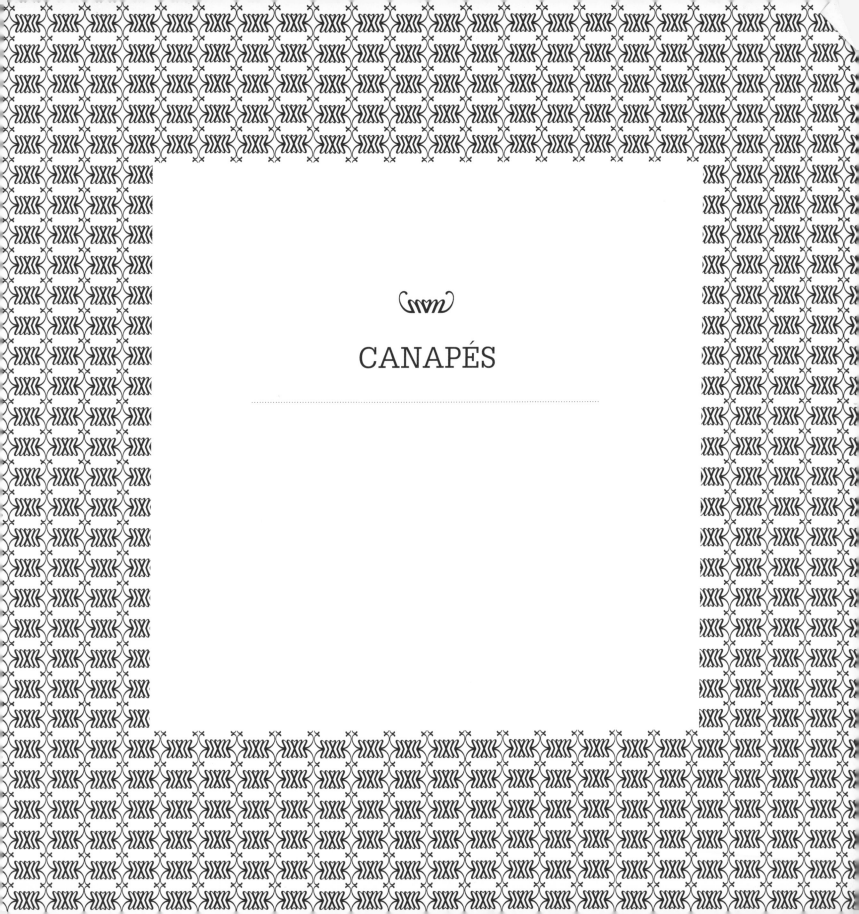

CANAPÉS

Tomato Gazpacho with Tomato Jelly

1 red pepper
1 small cucumber, peeled
½ red onion
1 kg vine-ripened tomatoes
10 basil leaves
1 teaspoon Tabasco sauce
1 tablespoon Worcestershire sauce
1 tablespoon castor sugar
2 tablespoons red-wine vinegar
1 tablespoon salt
1 gelatine leaf, softened in cold water
¼ bunch Greek basil or 10–15 small basil leaves

This refreshing palate cleanser is ideal to serve in the summer.

Finely dice about 1 tablespoon each of the red pepper, cucumber and onion and set aside. Roughly chop the rest of the red pepper, cucumber and onion then place in a food processor, along with all the remaining ingredients except the gelatine and Greek basil, and purée until smooth. Allow the mixture to sit for 1 hour then pass through a fine sieve into a bowl. Remove 250 ml of the gazpacho then cover the rest with plastic film and refrigerate until needed.

Place a muslin-lined sieve over a saucepan and pour the reserved 250 ml of gazpacho into the sieve, then leave to drip through – this should take about 1 hour, and the resulting liquid should be clear. (Do not force the liquid through, or it will become cloudy.) Place the saucepan over medium heat and bring the liquid to a simmer. Remove from the heat, add the softened gelatine and stir until it is completely dissolved. Divide this clear jelly between 10–15 shot glasses and refrigerate for 1 hour to set.

When ready to serve, pour the chilled gazpacho into the shot glasses, on top of the jelly. Mix together the reserved red pepper, cucumber and onion then sprinkle over the gazpacho, and garnish with Greek basil leaves.

Makes 10–15

Olive Bread with Goat's Cheese

1 loaf olive bread
250 g aged white-mould goat's cheese,
    such as St Maure de Touraine

Onion compote
30 g butter
2 onions, thinly sliced
1 tablespoon honey
2 tablespoons sherry vinegar
salt and pepper

I love the combination of flavours in this simple canapé. The saltiness of the olives is a perfect foil for the sweetness of the caramelised onions and the creamy richness of the goat's cheese. Served on top of a salad of rocket, semi-dried tomatoes and shaved fennel, these toasted olive bread canapés also make a great lunch for a lazy Sunday.

To make the onion compote, melt the butter in a saucepan and add the onion then reduce the heat to medium and cook, stirring constantly, until the onion starts to caramelise. Add the honey and continue cooking for about 30 minutes. Finish with the sherry vinegar and season with salt and pepper to taste.

Use a sharp bread knife to cut 4 mm slices of the olive bread, then cut each slice into 3 cm rounds or squares. Place under the grill and toast until a light golden colour. Cut the goat's cheese into slices, place a slice on each piece of toast, then top with a teaspoon of onion compote.

Makes 20

Tuna Pops with Red Curry Dressing

250 g yellowfin tuna
20 bamboo skewers
100 ml soy sauce

Red curry dressing
2 long red chillies
10 thin slices galangal
1 stalk lemongrass
10 cloves garlic

3 golden shallots
1 coriander root
2 tablespoons grapeseed oil
1 teaspoon white peppercorns, finely ground
1½ teaspoons shrimp paste
1½ teaspoons palm sugar
800 ml coconut cream
1 tablespoon fish sauce
baby coriander sprigs, to serve

I love these fish pops because they are fun, different and uncomplicated, yet they have an intense flavour. It is imperative that you use high-quality tuna, ideally yellowfin. I prefer to make the red curry dressing from scratch, but if you are pushed for time, you could buy a small can of red curry paste, then dilute it with some coconut cream and sweeten it with palm sugar to taste.

First, make the red curry dressing. Roughly chop the chillies, galangal, lemongrass, garlic, shallots and coriander root, then pound using a pestle and mortar, or blend with a hand-held blender, until you have a smooth paste. Heat the grapeseed oil in a heavy-based saucepan and gently fry 4 tablespoons of the curry paste, stirring constantly, until it becomes aromatic – about 3–5 minutes. Add the ground white peppercorns, shrimp paste, palm sugar, coconut cream and fish sauce and simmer until reduced by half. Pass the dressing through a fine sieve into a bowl.

Use a sharp knife to cut the tuna into 1.5 cm cubes, then spear each piece of tuna with a bamboo skewer.

Place the red curry dressing in a small dish on a serving platter and garnish with baby coriander. Just before serving, dip each 'tuna pop' into soy sauce and place on the platter.

Makes 20

Crab and Sweetcorn Soup

250 g cooked crab meat
6 corn cobs, husked
2 litres crab stock (see page 207)
1 small leek, white part only, well-washed and finely chopped
1 clove garlic, crushed
80 g salted butter

1 bay leaf
salt and pepper
200 ml cream
6 teaspoons shellfish oil (see page 211) – optional
Greek basil sprigs, to serve

I know what you're thinking – 'Why has he got a recipe for a soup that's found on every menu in every Chinese restaurant across the country?'. Well, the short answer is that this soup bears no resemblance to those. It is crucial that you use fresh corn, as frozen or tinned corn doesn't have the same sweet flavour. The sweetness of fresh corn helps accentuate the savoury flavour of the fresh crab meat (which is readily available in vacuum-sealed bags from most quality fishmongers). The shellfish oil, although not essential, does add colour and piquancy to the finished dish. Greek basil is a compact plant with smaller leaves that work well as a garnish, but if you can't find it, regular basil is fine.

About 30 minutes before serving, remove the crab meat from the refrigerator and leave to come to room temperature.

Place a corn cob upright on a chopping board, then, using a small sharp knife, cut downwards along the cob to remove the kernels. Repeat with the remaining cobs.

Place the crab stock in a large saucepan and bring to the boil; keep hot. Place the leek, garlic and butter in another large saucepan, then cook over medium heat, stirring frequently, until translucent. Add the bay leaf and corn kernels and cook for another 3–4 minutes, then lightly season with salt and pepper. Add the boiling stock to the corn mixture and simmer for 20 minutes or until the corn is tender. Add the cream, then remove from the heat. Process the corn mixture to a smooth purée in a blender or food processor, then pass through a fine sieve placed over a large saucepan and season to taste. Gently reheat the soup over medium heat until warmed through.

To serve, place a pile of crabmeat in the centre of six warmed bowls, then ladle over the sweetcorn soup. Drizzle with shellfish oil, if desired, and top with a Greek basil sprig.

Serves 6

Jerusalem Artichoke Soup

3 × 250 g whole live marrons *or* 300 g cooked lobster meat
2 litres chicken stock
80 g butter
½ leek, white part only, well-washed and finely chopped
2 cloves garlic, finely chopped
1 kg Jerusalem artichokes, peeled and finely chopped
salt and pepper

250 ml cream
shiso leaves and extra virgin olive oil, to serve

Artichoke chips
2 large or 3 smaller Jerusalem artichokes, peeled
vegetable oil, for deep-frying

I make this soup every winter, without fail. It has a nutty and creamy flavour that works a treat with marron or other shellfish. Try and buy the fattest Jerusalem artichokes you can find, since they can be fiddly to peel; as soon as they're peeled, place them in a bowl of water with a squeeze of lemon juice, to make sure they don't turn brown. While marron is a wonderful freshwater crustacean, most are destined for restaurants. However, I have made this dish and served it with prawns, lobster and even yabbies, and it still tastes great!

If using live marrons, place them in the freezer for 1 hour, then plunge them into boiling salted water for 4–5 minutes, remove and transfer to a large bowl of iced water to cool. Once cold, take the meat from the shells and thinly slice. If using freshly cooked lobster meat, simply cut into slices.

To make the artichoke chips, using a mandoline or large sharp knife, cut the artichokes into 1 mm slices. Deep-fry the artichoke slices in oil heated to 200°C in a deep-fryer or heavy-based saucepan for 2–3 minutes or until golden brown, then remove and drain on kitchen paper.

Place the chicken stock in a large saucepan and bring to the boil; keep hot. Melt the butter in a large saucepan, then add the leek and garlic and cook for 2–3 minutes or until translucent; do not allow to brown. Add the artichokes to the pan and season with salt and pepper to taste. Transfer the chicken stock to the artichoke mixture and then simmer for 10 minutes or until the artichokes are tender. Add the cream, stir, then process to a smooth purée using a hand-held blender. Pass the soup through a fine sieve placed over a large saucepan and season to taste. Gently reheat the soup over medium heat until warmed through.

To serve, divide the soup among six warmed shallow bowls. Place the sliced marron, lobster or prawn, shiso leaves and artichoke chips in the centre and drizzle with a few drops of extra virgin olive oil.

Serves 6

Butternut Pumpkin and Mussel Soup

1 litre chicken stock
50 g butter
50 ml olive oil
1 onion, finely chopped
pinch ground nutmeg
1.5 kg butternut pumpkin, peeled and cut into 1 cm dice
salt and pepper
120 g crème fraîche
finely chopped chives, to serve

Steamed mussels
30 ml olive oil
1 onion, finely chopped
2 cloves garlic, crushed
4 thyme sprigs
1 bay leaf
1.2 kg black mussels, scrubbed and debearded
200 ml white wine

Pumpkin soup is probably one of the most popular soups, and here I have added some steamed mussels and a dollop of crème fraîche. I love the contrast between the briny flavour of the mussels, the sweetness of the pumpkin and the sour edge of the crème fraîche. I prefer to use chicken stock for a fuller flavour, but if you want to make a vegetarian version, you could certainly use vegetable stock instead and leave out the shellfish.

For the steamed mussels, heat the olive oil in a large saucepan, then add the onion, garlic, thyme and bay leaf and stir. Add the mussels and white wine, then cook, covered, for 2–3 minutes or until the mussels just open, shaking the pan occasionally. Remove the mussels, then strain the cooking juices and set aside. When just cool enough to handle, remove the mussels from their shells and set aside in a covered bowl while you make the soup.

Place the chicken stock in a large saucepan and bring to the boil; keep hot. Melt the butter with the olive oil in another large saucepan over low heat, then add the onion and nutmeg and cook, stirring frequently, for 2–3 minutes or until the onion is translucent. Add the pumpkin, reserved mussel-cooking liquid and boiling chicken stock to the pan, then simmer, covered, for 30 minutes. Process the soup to a smooth purée using a hand-held blender, then pass through a fine sieve placed over a large saucepan and season to taste. Gently reheat the soup over medium heat until warmed through. If necessary, adjust the consistency with a little extra chicken stock.

Ladle the pumpkin soup into eight warmed bowls, top with the steamed mussels and a dollop of crème fraîche, then serve sprinkled with finely chopped chives.

Serves 8

SALADS & LIGHT MEALS

Baby Vegetable Salad with Persian Fetta and Hazelnut Dressing

12 cherry tomatoes
18 baby carrots
6 baby fennel
18 asparagus tips
75 g peas in pods, shelled
6 dill sprigs
6 chervil sprigs
6 chives
6 basil sprigs
3 zucchini (courgette) flowers, petals separated
35 g hazelnuts, roasted
200 g Persian fetta
salt and pepper

Hazelnut dressing
½ clove garlic, crushed
1 teaspoon Dijon mustard
25 ml chardonnay vinegar
55 ml honey
110 ml hazelnut oil
salt and pepper

This summer salad was inspired by a dish I ate in a Bali resort many years ago. I wanted to create a dish that was both elegant and simple. The dish has more of a visual impact if you can buy baby vegetables, but if you can only get regular-sized beetroot, carrots or fennel, that's fine – just cut them into similar sizes to those of the other vegetables. Only the delicate tips of the asparagus are used in this salad, but the rest of the spears can be added to a risotto (see page 67) or frittata (see page 52). Marinated in olive oil, herbs, garlic and peppercorns, Persian fetta is softer and less salty than regular fetta. Produced in Victoria's Yarra Valley, it is available from specialist cheese shops and some delicatessens. The herbs can be any of the soft variety, such as flat-leaf parsley, dill, chives, mint or basil, as long as they are the freshest you can find. The hint of sweetness in the hazelnut dressing is a perfect foil for the saltiness of the fetta. Store the leftover dressing in an airtight container in the fridge, where it will keep for 2–3 weeks, and use on salads.

Preheat the oven to 100°C. Arrange the cherry tomatoes on a baking tray and place in the oven for 2 hours or until semi-dried. Remove from the oven and leave to cool.

Bring a large saucepan of water to the boil and blanch the vegetables until just tender: the baby carrots and fennel will need about 3–5 minutes, while the asparagus tips and peas should only take 1–2 minutes. Drain the vegetables and refresh under cold running water.

To make the hazelnut dressing, combine the garlic, mustard, vinegar and honey in a bowl. Gradually whisk in the oil until emulsified, then season to taste with salt and pepper. >

Baby beetroot
3 teaspoons sugar
3 teaspoons white wine vinegar
6 baby beetroot, trimmed and scrubbed

Saffron potatoes
3 medium-sized kipfler potatoes, peeled
pinch saffron threads
salt

Shimeji mushrooms
125 ml rice wine vinegar
35 g sugar
1 clove
½ teaspoon mustard seeds
3 black peppercorns
½ teaspoon finely chopped ginger
1 bird's eye chilli, cut in half and deseeded
¼ clove garlic, finely chopped
60 g shimeji mushrooms

To prepare the baby beetroot, place the sugar, vinegar and 500 ml of water in a saucepan and bring to the boil. Add the beetroot and simmer for 10–15 minutes or until tender, then leave to cool in the liquid. When they are cool enough to handle, peel the beetroot with your fingers (use disposable gloves if you want to avoid stained hands!), then cut them into quarters.

For the saffron potatoes, place the potatoes, saffron and a generous pinch of salt in a saucepan with plenty of water. Bring to the boil and cook the potatoes for 10–15 minutes or until tender. Leave to cool, then cut into 1 cm slices.

To prepare the shimeji mushrooms, place all the ingredients except the mushrooms in a saucepan, add 250 ml water and bring to the boil. Add the mushrooms, then immediately remove from the heat and leave the mushrooms to cool in the liquid before draining.

Very gently toss the vegetables, mushrooms, herbs, zucchini flowers and hazelnuts together in a bowl with 2 tablespoons of the hazelnut dressing, then arrange on a large plate. Crumble the fetta over the vegetables, drizzle with a little more of the hazelnut dressing and season to taste with salt and pepper.

Serves 6

wine
A chilled bottle of medium-bodied chardonnay from either the Barossa or Coonawarra is a good match. Chardonnays from these warmer regions are generally quite ripe, almost tasting of peaches and cream. They also have vanilla and toasted-nut characters, which echo the nutty flavour of the dressing.

Fig, Baby Bean, Prosciutto, Blue Cheese and Rocket Salad

250 g baby green beans, trimmed
25 ml olive oil
25 ml aged balsamic vinegar
50 g rocket

10 slices prosciutto
6 black figs, quartered
50 g blue cheese, crumbled
salt and pepper

This is a simple rustic salad: if you use good-quality ingredients, you can't go wrong. Choose figs which are plump, heavy and almost splitting at the base. Although this is normally a sign that fruit has deteriorated, in the case of figs it is the best indicator that they are ripe, jammy and full of juice. The beans should be quickly blanched and refreshed so they are still vibrant green and crunchy. The sweet flavour of figs marries effortlessly with the sharp, assertive bite of blue cheese – I have used the French Fourme d'Ambert, but gorgonzola or Roquefort would also be good. The dressing is made with aged balsamic vinegar, which has a round and slightly sweet flavour that contrasts well with the acidity of the blue cheese.

Place the beans in a saucepan of boiling water and cook for 2–3 minutes. Drain and refresh under cold running water.

Whisk together the olive oil and balsamic vinegar to make a dressing. Place the beans and rocket in a bowl and toss with 2 tablespoons of the dressing.

Place the dressed beans and rocket on a platter. Fold the prosciutto slices and arrange over the beans and rocket, together with the figs and blue cheese. Drizzle the salad with a little more dressing and season to taste.

Serves 6

wine

There are two wine options here: one would be a bone-dry fino sherry, which has a slightly salty mineral flavour; the other, a glass of chilled barsac. This sweet French wine is similar in flavour to the more famous sauternes. Best served very cold, it has a wonderful flavour of orange blossom and apricots, balanced by a distinctive note of almonds and iced marzipan.

Warm Salad of Mozzarella and Asparagus

18 truss cherry tomatoes, stems intact
rock salt
24 asparagus spears, trimmed
6 × 125 g buffalo mozzarella balls, at room temperature
½ head curly endive, leaves picked
½ bunch chervil, leaves picked

salsa verde (see page 210) and aged balsamic vinegar, to serve
salt and pepper

Croûtons
1 small loaf sourdough bread
olive oil

For this dish, I love to use imported Italian 100 per cent buffalo milk mozzarella, which has a fabulous creamy texture and nutty flavour, but you can of course use an Australian mozzarella instead. It is also important to only heat the mozzarella through, say for 3–4 minutes or until the edges just start to melt slightly. If heated any longer, the texture becomes too elastic and stringy. Look for an aged balsamic vinegar that's at least seven years old, as it will have a sweeter, smoother flavour. This is the epitome of a modern Italian dish, where the quality of the core ingredients allows them to speak for themselves. *Buon appetito!*

To make the croûtons, thinly slice the bread, then cut rustic chunks of the crust only. (Rather than waste the rest of the loaf, pulse it in a food processor or blender to make breadcrumbs and freeze them for later use.) Cover the base of a hot frying pan with a little olive oil, then shallow-fry the bread chunks over medium heat for approximately 2–3 minutes or until golden brown. Drain on kitchen paper and set aside.

Preheat the oven to 150°C. To roast the cherry tomatoes, spread a 1 cm layer of rock salt over the base of a roasting tin and top with the tomatoes. Place in the oven and roast for approximately 15 minutes, or until the tomatoes are very slightly blistered but still holding their shape.

Meanwhile, blanch the asparagus: place in boiling water for 1–2 minutes, then refresh under cold running water and drain.

When ready to serve, place the mozzarella balls under a hot grill for 3–4 minutes, or until they start to melt slightly around the edges and brown a little. Place the mozzarella in the centre of a large plate, then arrange the asparagus, tomatoes, croûtons, endive and chervil around the cheese. Finish with the salsa verde and drops of aged balsamic vinegar around the edges. Season with salt and pepper and serve immediately.

Serves 6

wine

To maintain this salad's Italianate theme, I'd suggest an Italian white wine. The quality of Italian white wine has lifted enormously over the last 15 years. For instance, white wines from Sicily that blend the local greciano grape with newly planted chardonnay grapes are rich, but balanced with an intense citrus acidity that complements the fresh mozzarella. These wines also commonly exude aromas of fresh green herbs and asparagus, matching the flavours of this salad beautifully.

Croque Monsieur and Croque Madame

360 g crème fraîche
300 g gruyère, grated
50 g Dijon mustard
salt and pepper to taste
16 slices thick-cut white bread
8 slices leg ham

For Croque Madame
8 eggs
butter, for frying

These toasted cheese and ham sandwiches are my number-one favourite brunch dish. The sandwiches can be made up ahead of time, so that all you need to do when you're ready to serve is put them in the oven to warm through and then brown them under the grill. The difference between a Croque Monsieur and a Croque Madame is that a Croque Madame has a fried egg placed on top just as it comes out of the oven. The sight of freshly laid eggs always brings back childhood memories of running around the farm and collecting eggs from the hen house. Now that I am a father, I love to see my young son Harry running excitedly to gather the eggs, just as I did.

Preheat the oven to 200°C.

In a bowl, mix the crème fraîche, gruyère cheese and Dijon mustard together then season with salt and pepper. Spread a layer of this mixture on one side of two slices of bread, put a slice of ham on the top of one of the slices and then put the other slice on top, with the cheese-side facing up. Repeat with the remaining slices of bread and cheese mixture.

Lay the sandwiches on a baking tray and place in the oven for 10 minutes.

If making Croque Madame, melt a small knob of butter in a hot, non-stick frying pan over medium heat and fry the eggs for 2–3 minutes. Depending on the size of your frying pan, you may need to do this in two or more batches.

Remove the sandwiches from the oven and place under a hot grill until golden brown. Serve immediately – as is for Croque Monsieur, or topped with a fried egg for Croque Madame.

Serves 8

wine
Considering these toasted sandwiches are perfect for a weekend brunch, I would serve a spicy bloody mary, with plenty of ice and a stick of celery.

Tuna Niçoise Salad

400 g sashimi-quality tuna, cut into logs 5 cm in diameter
salt and pepper
olive oil
1 bunch chervil, finely chopped
1 bunch coriander, finely chopped
1 bunch flat-leaf parsley, finely chopped
6 kipfler potatoes
200 g baby beans
9 quail eggs
9 small cherry tomatoes
1 bunch basil, leaves picked

30 g anchovy fillets, preferably Ortiz
100 g pesto (see page 209)
100 g mayonnaise (see page 209)
sea salt flakes and cracked black pepper, to serve

Tapenade
2 golden shallots, finely chopped
1 clove garlic, chopped
150 g kalamata olives, pitted
12 g salted capers, rinsed and drained
12 g anchovy fillets, preferably Ortiz

This iconic salad is beautiful to look at, and even more beautiful to eat. Buy high-quality yellowfin tuna, or even bluefin, if you can find it, and ask your fishmonger to cut the tuna into one or more 5 cm diameter logs. Tuna should always be crimson red in colour with a bright sheen; it should be firm with no separations, and should not be slimy to the touch. But don't fret if you don't have time to buy fresh tuna or to make your own mayonnaise – as long as you get good-quality mayonnaise and the best tinned tuna, you'll still have a delectable salad that makes a perfect light lunch.

Season the tuna generously with salt and pepper. Heat a little olive oil in a medium-hot non-stick frying pan and sear the tuna logs for 20–30 seconds, then remove and leave to cool. Place the combined chopped herbs on a plate and roll the tuna in the herbs, pressing down to coat evenly. Tightly wrap the herb-coated tuna in plastic film and refrigerate for 1 hour. Remove the plastic film and cut the tuna into six even slices.

Meanwhile, to make the tapenade, process all the ingredients in a food processor until smooth.

Place the potatoes in a saucepan, cover with cold water and bring to the boil, then simmer for 10–15 minutes or until tender. Remove, allow to cool slightly, then peel and cut into 1 cm slices. Blanch the baby beans in a saucepan of boiling water for 2–3 minutes, then refresh under cold running water. Place the quail eggs in a small saucepan of boiling water, and cook for 2 minutes 20 seconds, until semi-soft (the yolks should still be slightly runny). Leave in cold water to cool slightly, then shell and cut in half. Cut the cherry tomatoes in half.

Arrange the potatoes, beans, basil leaves, cherry tomatoes and anchovy fillets on six plates. Add dollops of pesto, mayonnaise and tapenade to each salad. Arrange the quail eggs and tuna on top, seasoning it with a little sea salt and cracked pepper.

Serves 6

wine
I have served this dish at home many times, and tend to think that a white wine which has some savoury flavours is the best match. I suggest a marsanne–roussanne blend from either the Goulburn Valley in New South Wales or Victoria's Yarra Valley. These blends typically have richer flavours that include hints of tobacco, toast, nuts, honey and nectarine.

Zucchini, Leek and Mushroom Frittata

20 g butter
2 tablespoons olive oil
½ leek, white part only, well-washed and diced
1 clove garlic, crushed
80 g zucchini (courgettes), coarsely grated
50 g button mushrooms, sliced

100 ml milk
6 eggs
salt and pepper
1 tablespoon thyme leaves
40 g freshly grated pecorino

Frittata can be served with a simple green salad as a brunch or light lunch dish, or cut into wedges as part of an antipasto platter. Don't be afraid to substitute ingredients in this frittata recipe – you could use asparagus instead of zucchini, onions instead of leeks, or peppers instead of mushrooms. The only things you need to be careful of are to chop your chosen ingredients to a uniform, small size so that they become evenly distributed through the egg mixture and will cook evenly, and to use a non-stick pan so your frittata will slide out effortlessly every time.

In a non-stick frying pan, melt the butter with the olive oil then add the leek, garlic, grated zucchini and mushrooms and fry over medium heat until the vegetables are soft; season lightly.

Pour the milk into a bowl, break the eggs into the milk and beat lightly, seasoning to taste. Add the egg and milk mixture to the frying pan and cook over medium heat, lifting the edges and bringing them into the middle as the frittata starts to set. This allows some air under the mixture. Turn the heat down and cook until the eggs are just set – this should take about 3–4 minutes. To flip the frittata, hold a plate larger than the frying pan over the top of the pan, then invert the pan to turn out the frittata onto the plate. Carefully slide the frittata back into the frying pan and cook for another 2–3 minutes to brown the other side.

To serve, ease the frittata onto a warmed plate, then sprinkle with thyme leaves and freshly grated pecorino.

Serves 6

wine
I would recommend a fresh and lively current-release sauvignon blanc. The Adelaide Hills region of South Australia produces sauvignon blanc that has a perfume of gooseberries and lychees, with a crisp, dry finish.

Caramelised Shallot Tarte Tatin with Goat's Cheese

500 g golden shallots, peeled
250 g castor sugar
30 g cultured unsalted butter
200 ml sherry vinegar
2 puff pastry sheets
30 baby leeks
120 g goat's cheese
6 tablespoons salsa verde (see page 210)
sea salt flakes and chervil, to serve

Sauce
300 g golden shallots, sliced
60 g cultured unsalted butter
2 cloves garlic, peeled
100 ml cream
salt and pepper

Vinaigrette
50 ml chardonnay vinegar
50 ml champagne vinegar
juice of ½ lemon, strained
1 tablespoon Dijon mustard

This is a favourite vegetarian dish of mine. It is important to use soft fresh goat's cheese; I like Jannei Buche Noir, but goat's curd or ricotta would work equally well. Tarte tatin moulds are specially designed round shallow baking tins, and they are available from kitchenware shops – try to find individual non-stick ones about 9 cm in diameter.

First, make the sauce. Blanch the sliced shallots in boiling water for 2 minutes and refresh in a sieve under cold running water. Put the butter and garlic in a saucepan with the shallots and cook until soft and tender, but do not allow to brown. In a separate saucepan, bring the cream to the boil, then add to the shallots. Season to taste, allow the sauce to cool slightly then purée in a food processor. For a smoother consistency, strain the sauce through a sieve after puréeing. Set aside until ready to serve.

To make the tatin, blanch the whole shallots in boiling salted water for about 6–8 minutes, or until tender. Strain and allow to cool slightly, then remove the outside layer from each shallot with your fingers. Place the sugar in a saucepan and stir constantly over medium heat until the sugar melts and begins to caramelise. Add the butter and stir until the mixture is golden brown. Add the whole shallots and sherry vinegar and continue cooking and stirring until the caramel coats the shallots – about 5–6 minutes. Transfer to a bowl and leave to cool. Preheat the oven to 180°C. Lay out the pastry on the bench, then use a 9 cm circular cutter to cut out six discs. When the caramelised shallots are cool, arrange them neatly in six 9 cm tarte tatin moulds placed on a baking sheet, then pour a spoonful of caramel syrup over the top of each. Lay the pastry discs on top, pressing around the edges to seal, then brush with melted butter. Bake for 15–18 minutes.

While the tarts are baking, make the vinaigrette by whisking all the ingredients together in a small bowl until emulsified, and gently reheat the sauce. Blanch the leeks in a saucepan of salted boiling water for 2–3 minutes, then refresh under cold running water.

Turn out the tarts, shallot-side up, on a baking sheet, place a slice of goat's cheese on top of each one and return to the oven for 3–4 minutes. Pour some sauce onto each warmed plate and then place a tart on top. Serve the leeks to one side, dressed with a little vinaigrette and a spoonful of salsa verde. Sprinkle with a little sea salt and garnish with a sprig of chervil, if desired.

Serves 6

wine
A glass of aged Hunter Valley semillon or aged Clare Valley riesling would complement this dish. These wines have flavours of citrus, buttered toast and roasted nuts – a perfect match!

PASTA, RISOTTO & GNOCCHI

Taglierini with Green Vegetables and Butter

350 g fresh pasta dough (see page 209)
a little olive oil
120 g broccoli florets
120 g green beans, trimmed
120 g sugar snap peas (mange-tout), trimmed

2 bunches asparagus, cut into 2 cm lengths
125 g butter (cultured, if possible)
1 clove garlic, crushed
salt and pepper
30 g parmesan

I started serving this dish 15 years ago in my first restaurant, The Paddington Inn Bistro. It is perfect for a simple Sunday lunch, as it is quick and easy to prepare – and kids love it. To make it even quicker, use 350 g dried taglierini. The quality of the dish depends on using the freshest green vegetables and the finest parmesan you can get your hands on.

Roll out the pasta to number 1 on your pasta machine and then cut into fine 2 mm strips to make taglierini. Cook the pasta in a large saucepan of boiling water with a little olive oil added to it for 2–3 minutes or until al dente, then drain. If using ready-made pasta, cook for the time indicated on the packet.

Bring a large saucepan of water to the boil and blanch the vegetables until just tender: the broccoli and beans will need about 2–3 minutes, while the sugar snap peas and asparagus should only take 1–2 minutes. Drain the vegetables and refresh under cold running water.

Melt the butter in a large saucepan over low heat. Add the garlic and cook until soft without browning, then add all the blanched vegetables and stir for 2–3 minutes until heated through. Add the pasta to the pan and toss with the vegetables. Season to taste and finish with freshly shaved parmesan.

Serves 6–8

wine
A glass of sauvignon blanc or a semillon–sauvignon blanc blend is a great partner for this dish. These types of wines have flavours of fresh green herbs, peas and asparagus, which directly echo the ingredients in this dish. I would opt for a medium-bodied sauvignon blend, with some toasty, nutty, barrel-ferment characters.

Truffled Poached Egg with Stracci Pasta

2 bunches green asparagus, trimmed
350 g fresh pasta dough (see page 209)
4 eggs, infused with truffles for 24–48 hours
2 tablespoons white wine vinegar

40 g cold salted butter, diced
8 g black truffle
salt and pepper
40 g parmesan

I am a self-confessed truffle maniac: I find their beguiling musky odour unique and very powerful. Yes, they are incredibly expensive, at $2000–3000 per kilogram, but they are a special treat for that ultimate decadent dinner party you should have at least once in your life. Fresh truffles may be stored for about two weeks in the refrigerator.

The best way to get value out of your truffles is to store them with eggs in an airtight container in the fridge for a day or two to infuse or 'truffle' the eggs. These truffle-infused eggs can then be poached, scrambled or fried. (Truffle-infused eggs can also be purchased at The Essential Ingredient stores in Melbourne and Sydney.)

In this recipe, a truffled poached egg is placed on top of the pasta: when the yolk is broken, it combines with the nut-brown butter and is transformed into an unctuous golden sauce that coats the pasta. The truffle itself can be shaved over the top of risotto, soup or pasta.

Roll out the pasta to number 1 on your pasta machine and then cut into 2 cm wide strips to make stracci.

To poach the truffle-infused eggs, fill a saucepan with water and add the vinegar. Bring it to the boil then reduce to a simmer until bubbles can just be seen rising. Break each egg into a cup, stir the water with a spoon to create a whirlpool then slip in the egg. (Depending on the size of your pan, you may need to cook the eggs in two batches.) Poach the eggs for 2–3 minutes or until just set; do not allow the yolk to harden.

Meanwhile, cook the pasta and asparagus in separate pans of salted boiling water for 1–2 minutes, or until the asparagus is just tender and the pasta is al dente, then drain. Return the pasta to the pan. Cut asparagus into 2 cm lengths, add to the pasta and gently toss together.

Heat a small frying pan until hot, add the cold butter and cook until the butter foams and turns nut-brown.

Divide the pasta and asparagus among four shallow bowls. Place a poached egg on top and shave the truffle directly onto the egg. Drizzle with the nut-brown butter, season then finish with freshly grated parmesan and serve immediately.

Serves 4

wine
This indulgent dish demands a decadent wine. A complex pinot noir from New Zealand or a premier cru red burgundy would be ideal. The wine should be medium-bodied, soft and not too tannic – an Italian barbaresco or a gamay from the Burgundy region would be good alternatives.

SEAFOOD

Oysters with Chardonnay Dressing

rock salt
48 oysters, freshly shucked
100 g ocean trout roe
1 bunch chives, finely chopped
3 lemons, cut in half

Chardonnay dressing
225 ml chardonnay
50 g castor sugar
150 ml chardonnay vinegar, preferably Forum
12 golden shallots, finely diced

The most important consideration with oysters is that they are freshly shucked. However, it can take years to perfect the art of oyster shucking, so I suggest you ask your fishmonger to open up your oysters in front of you. Not only will you know how long they have been shucked, but also all the natural juices can be left to sit in the shell. I prefer Sydney rock oysters, as I find they have a more intense salty flavour and are generally not too large. No matter what variety you choose, always look for oysters that sit full and plump in the shell, with an appealing shine. Another quick tip: don't serve your oysters too cold, or their wonderful briny flavour will be stunted.

The dressing may be refrigerated for up to one month, and can also used to dress salads or as a base for sauces.

For the chardonnay dressing, place the chardonnay and sugar in a small saucepan, then bring to the boil. Flambé the liquid in the saucepan – that is, set it alight to burn off the alcohol. Then wait until the flame goes out, remove from the heat and set aside to cool. Add the chardonnay vinegar and shallots to the cooled liquid, then leave to marinate for 3–4 hours.

To serve, place a bed of rock salt on each plate, then top with 8 freshly shucked oysters. Spoon a teaspoon of the dressing over each oyster, then top each with ½ teaspoon of ocean trout roe and finish with finely chopped chives. Place a lemon half, wrapped in muslin if desired, in the centre.

Serves 6

wine

Champagne! Champagne! Champagne! There really is only one drink that is the perfect partner with oysters, and that is this effervescent and savoury wine from France. If you can't get your hands on French Champagne, some Australian sparkling wines, such as Croser, Jansz and Yarrabank, are world-class – and a lot more affordable. Cheers!

Citrus-cured Salmon with Fennel and Orange Salad

100 g salt
150 g sugar
finely grated zest of 1 lime
finely grated zest of 1 orange
finely grated zest of 1 lemon
20 coriander seeds
20 white peppercorns
1 cup finely chopped dill
900 g salmon fillet, skin-on, pin-boned
2 teaspoons Dijon mustard
1 small fennel bulb
3 oranges
rocket, to serve

Honey and mustard dressing
1 tablespoon yellow mustard seeds
30 ml chardonnay vinegar
1 tablespoon honey
1 tablespoon Dijon mustard
½ clove garlic, crushed
150 ml grapeseed oil
1 tablespoon lemon juice
salt and pepper

I love this dish as a starter – the refreshing flavours of fennel and oranges are perfectly complemented by the honey and mustard dressing. The two important points to bear in mind are: firstly, make sure you don't cure the salmon for more than 24 hours or it will become too dry; secondly, use a very sharp, long knife to help you slice the salmon as thinly as possible. I always make a little more cured salmon than I need, as my young son, Harry, loves it on his sandwiches that he takes to school.

To cure the salmon, mix together the salt, sugar, citrus zests, coriander seeds, white peppercorns and 5 tablespoons of the dill in a bowl. With a sharp knife, cut 5–6 incisions on the skin-side of the salmon (make sure there are no fine bones in the salmon – use kitchen tweezers to remove any stray ones). Place the salmon on a large plate, cover with the salt mixture, then cover with plastic film and refrigerate for 24 hours.

The next day, remove the cured salmon from the fridge and rinse off the salt mixture under cold running water, then pat dry with kitchen paper. Smear a thin layer of Dijon mustard over the salmon, cover with the remaining dill, then wrap firmly in plastic film. Press between two baking trays in the refrigerator for 2 hours.

To make the dressing, place the mustard seeds and vinegar in a small bowl and leave for 30 minutes. In another bowl, whisk together the honey, Dijon mustard, garlic and oil until emulsified. Whisk in the vinegar-soaked mustard seeds, lemon juice and 30 ml of water, then season to taste.

Trim the fennel, reserving the fronds, then slice the fennel bulb into paper-thin slices (a Japanese mandoline is great for a job like this). Peel the oranges and cut into segments, avoiding the pith. Place the fennel slices and orange segments in a bowl, toss with some of the dressing, then season to taste.

When ready to serve, remove the salmon from the plastic film, and, using a long sharp knife, slice thinly. Lay the slices on one side of the plate, then place the salad on the other side, drizzle with a little more dressing and garnish with the reserved fennel fronds and some rocket leaves.

Serves 6

wine
A light- to medium-bodied rosé or pinot noir, with good acidity and flavours of strawberries and raspberries, is ideal with this.

Tuna Sashimi with Wasabi Avocado and Daikon Dressing

30 g enoki mushrooms
450 g sashimi-grade yellowfin tuna
½ cucumber, peeled and cut into 5 cm strips
60 g daikon, peeled and cut into 5 cm strips
¼ cup baby coriander leaves
1 teaspoon black sesame seeds

Daikon dressing
1 tablespoon sesame oil
100 ml rice wine vinegar
40 ml mirin

50 ml light soy sauce
30 g daikon, peeled and grated
1 teaspoon finely diced ginger

Wasabi avocado
2 tablespoons sugar
1 avocado, peeled and stone removed
juice of 1 lime
1 teaspoon wasabi powder
1 cucumber
20 g ocean trout roe

I love the simplicity of Japanese cuisine. This dish consists purely of the very best sashimi-grade bluefin or yellowfin tuna, cut perfectly and dressed with an aromatic Japanese dressing redolent with the flavours of ginger and daikon. Try to avoid serving any sashimi too cold, as the low temperature will stunt the delicate flavour of the raw fish. Black sesame seeds are available from health food shops and Asian supermarkets, but white sesame seeds will do if you can't find them.

For the daikon dressing, combine all the ingredients in a bowl and leave for 20 minutes to infuse. Strain through a sieve placed over a small bowl and set aside.

To make the wasabi avocado, place sugar in a small saucepan with 2 tablespoons water and bring to the boil, stirring to dissolve the sugar. Allow to cool slightly, then transfer to a food processor, along with the avocado, lime juice and wasabi powder, and blend until smooth.

Using a vegetable peeler, cut six fine strips of cucumber approximately 1 cm wide and form each strip into a circle on a tray lined with baking paper. Fill each cucumber circle with wasabi avocado and top with a little ocean trout roe.

Blanch the enoki mushrooms in a saucepan of boiling water for 30 seconds, then refresh under cold running water. Trim the tuna and cut into thin slices. Combine the mushrooms, cucumber, daikon and baby coriander in a large bowl, then place some salad on each plate. Drizzle over the daikon dressing, then arrange tuna slices on top, followed by an avocado-filled cucumber circle. Scatter with sesame seeds and serve immediately.

Serves 6

wine
In keeping with the Japanese flavours, I would recommend a small glass of chilled sake.

Chilli-salt Squid and Brandade

12 quail eggs
300 g whole squid, cleaned
peanut oil, for deep-frying
rocket, black olives and chilli oil (see page 207), to serve

Brandade
100 g table salt
2 thyme sprigs
2 bay leaves
2 rosemary sprigs
3 cloves garlic, chopped
250 g blue-eye trevalla fillet, skin removed and pin-boned
250 ml milk
250 ml cream

3 tablespoons finely grated parmesan
2 tablespoons strained lemon juice
4 tablespoons olive oil
2 tablespoons truffle oil
200 g mashed potato (see page 208)
salt and pepper

Chilli salt
2 tablespoons onion powder
2 tablespoons garlic powder
2 teaspoons chilli powder
180 g tempura flour
3 teaspoons fine salt
2 teaspoons freshly ground black pepper

Everyone loves chilli-salt squid, but I really like this recipe for its spicy salt mix with a complex smoky flavour that highlights the sweetness of the squid. Tempura flour is readily available from Asian supermarkets. If you have any chilli salt left over, simply store it in an airtight container, ready for your next batch of chilli-salt squid. Brandade is a purée of poached salted cod – I tend to keep its texture quite soft in this recipe, to contrast with the crisp fried squid. Quail eggs are lovely in this dish, but you can use six chicken eggs instead; just make sure the yolks stay runny. The rocket and olives add pepper and piquancy, and the chilli oil links all the ingredients together – a perfect combination! Any leftover chilli oil can be kept in a sealed container in a cool, dark place for up to 2 weeks. It is great drizzled over chargrilled fish or in pasta dishes.

To make the brandade, combine the salt, thyme, bay leaves, rosemary and garlic in a bowl. Place the trevalla on a large plate, cover with the salt mixture and leave for 1 hour in the fridge. Rinse the trevalla under cold running water, then pat dry with kitchen paper. Place the milk and cream in a saucepan and bring to a simmer, add the trevalla and poach, uncovered, for 4–5 minutes, then drain the fish, reserving the liquid. Place the fish in a bowl, then add the remaining ingredients and mix together, using a fork to break the fish into flakes. Season the brandade to taste with salt and pepper; if you would like it a little moister, just add a little of the cooking liquid. Cover and keep warm.

For perfect soft-boiled quail eggs, bring a saucepan of water to the boil, then carefully add the eggs. Boil for 2 minutes 20 seconds, then refresh in a bowl of iced water. When the eggs are cool enough to handle, shell them and return the eggs to the iced water.

To make the chilli-salt, simply mix all the ingredients together in a medium-sized bowl. Prepare the squid by removing the tentacles and cutting them in half crossways. Cut open the squid tubes, score the insides in a cross-hatch pattern, then cut into diamond-shaped pieces. Toss the squid through the chilli-salt, then deep-fry in peanut oil heated to 200°C in a deep-fryer or heavy-based saucepan for 2 minutes, or until crisp and golden. Remove and drain on kitchen paper.

To serve, place a spoonful of warm brandade on each plate, arrange the rocket and olives alongside and place the squid on top of the salad. Reheat the quail eggs in boiling water for 30 seconds, cut in half and place four halves on each plate. Finish with a drizzle of chilli oil and serve immediately.

Serves 6

wine
Spicy food is normally better complemented by aromatic white wines that have a little residual sugar. A floral gewurztraminer with flavours of roses, lychees and musk is a great match.

Scampi with Celeriac and a Scampi Bisque

Scampi bisque
olive oil and butter, for frying
1 carrot, peeled and finely chopped
2 celery stalks, finely chopped
1 leek, white part only, well-washed and finely chopped
1 onion, finely chopped
1 medium-sized fennel bulb, trimmed and finely chopped
1 clove garlic, chopped
1 tablespoon fennel seeds
1 tablespoon coriander seeds
1 star anise
3 tablespoons tomato paste
500 g prawn heads and shells *or* 250 g raw prawns
500 g scampi heads

60 ml brandy
1 cup white wine
4 egg tomatoes, roughly chopped
1.5 litres chicken stock
½ bunch tarragon
¼ bunch thyme
½ bunch coriander
2 bay leaves
½ bunch flat-leaf parsley
½ bunch basil
juice of ½ lemon
30 ml cream

This dish showcases the wonderful sweetness of scampi. It is important to watch the cooking time of the scampi: they only need to turn opaque and they are ready; if overcooked, they will become tough and rubbery. The bisque sauce reinforces the crustacean flavour, and it all sits upon a crab and celeriac remoulade (the word 'remoulade' is a French culinary term for something that is bound in mayonnaise). In order to make the stock for the bisque, you'll need to either build up a store of prawn heads and shells in your freezer, or substitute 250 g whole prawns – and don't forget to keep the scampi heads for the stockpot.

First, make the scampi bisque. Place a little olive oil and butter in a large saucepan and melt the butter, then add the carrot, celery, leek, onion, fennel, garlic, fennel seeds, coriander seeds and star anise and cook, stirring frequently, for 3–4 minutes or until tender; do not allow to brown. Add the tomato paste and the prawn and scampi heads. Pour in 50 ml of the brandy and carefully set it alight (to burn off the alcohol), then add the white wine, tomatoes, chicken stock, tarragon, thyme, coriander and bay leaves. Bring to the boil, then reduce the heat and simmer for 50 minutes. Strain the stock through a very fine sieve placed over a large saucepan. Add the parsley, basil and lemon juice, then set aside for 15 minutes to allow the flavours to infuse. Strain the stock again through a fine sieve placed over a clean saucepan, then reduce over high heat for about 20 minutes – the stock should become thick enough to coat the back of a spoon. Add the cream to the reduced stock and simmer until the sauce is reduced by approximately half. Stir in the remaining 10 ml of brandy, then set aside until ready to serve. >

Smoked Salmon Terrine with Pickled Beetroot Salad

550 g thinly sliced smoked salmon
420 g fromage blanc
2 nori sheets
baby rocket cress and extra virgin olive oil, to serve
salt and pepper

Smoked salmon mousse
250 g smoked salmon
350 ml cream
finely grated zest of 1 lemon
salt and pepper

Pickled beetroot
1 litre pickling mix (see page 209)
2 large beetroot

This terrine looks incredible on the plate and tastes just as good; any leftovers are lovely eaten with some crusty bread. Fromage blanc is a simple fresh cheese; if it isn't available, you can easily substitute mascarpone. The nori (seaweed) sheets can be bought from speciality Asian food stores.

First, make the smoked salmon mousse. Place the smoked salmon in a food processor and blend until smooth, then add the cream and blend again until smooth. Add the lemon zest and season to taste. Remove from the food processor and push through a fine sieve placed over a bowl, then place in a piping bag and refrigerate until needed.

To assemble the terrine, line a 29 × 9 cm terrine mould with plastic film, allowing about an extra 5 cm all around, then line with some of the smoked salmon slices, again allowing about 5 cm all around to overhang the edges of the mould. Spoon a thin layer of fromage blanc on top of the smoked salmon in the base of the terrine mould, smoothing it with the back of a spoon. Cut nori sheets in three to fit the terrine mould. Lay two pieces of nori on top of the fromage blanc, then pipe over a layer of smoked salmon mousse, again smoothing it with the back of a spoon, and top with some more slices of smoked salmon. Repeat these layers until the terrine mould is full. Fold over the overhanging smoked salmon and plastic film to cover the top layer, then press down

lightly, to remove any air pockets. Refrigerate for 8–10 hours. To remove the terrine from the mould, peel back the top layer of plastic film and use this to carefully lift out the terrine.

To make the pickled beetroot, place the pickling mix in a saucepan and bring to the boil, then add the beetroot and simmer for 30–40 minutes or until tender. Remove from the heat and set aside to cool. Peel the beetroot with your fingers (use disposable gloves if you want to avoid stained hands!), then cut into 1 cm dice. This can be done in advance: if the diced beetroot is stored in the cooking liquid in the refrigerator, it will keep for 6–8 weeks; just drain before using.

When ready to serve, combine the pickled beetroot and baby rocket cress leaves in a bowl and dress with a little olive oil, then season to taste. Using a wet, sharp knife, slice the terrine, making sure to remove the plastic film after slicing. Place a slice of terrine on each plate, with some beetroot salad to the side.

Serves 12

wine
I recommend an Alsatian pinot gris from France – a rich and full-bodied wine, with flavours of spiced pears and honey.

Seared Scallops with Creamed Corn

18 basil leaves
vegetable oil, for deep-frying
18 large scallops
salt and pepper
300 g sesame seaweed or
    300 g blanched spinach leaves
shellfish oil (see page 211), to serve – optional

Creamed corn
8 corn cobs, husked
70 g butter
½ medium-sized leek, white part only,
    well-washed and finely chopped
2 cloves garlic, crushed
100 ml chicken stock
250 ml cream
salt and pepper

All the work for this dish is in the preparation: the corn purée, dressed seaweed, deep-fried basil leaves and the shellfish oil are all done ahead of time. Available from some Asian food stores, sesame seaweed is a ready-made salad of seaweed, sesame seeds and chilli. If you can't find it, substitute blanched spinach leaves. While the shellfish oil is not an essential component, it does add depth to the dish and allows all the flavours to meld together. If you do decide to make it, bear in mind that this needs to be done at least 3–4 days in advance; the leftover shellfish oil can then be kept in a sealed glass bottle in the fridge for up to 2 weeks, and can be used to enhance seafood soups, salads and pasta dishes.

Deep-fry the basil leaves in vegetable oil heated to 170°C in a deep-fryer or saucepan for 5 seconds, or until crisp. Remove and drain on kitchen paper.

For the creamed corn, hold each corn cob upright on a chopping board and, using a small sharp knife, cut downwards in sections, following the contour of the cob, to remove the kernels. Heat the butter in a saucepan, then add the leek and garlic and cook over low heat until translucent; do not allow to colour. Add the corn kernels, chicken stock and cream, then season to taste with salt and pepper. Bring to the boil, then reduce the heat and simmer for approximately 10 minutes or until tender. Process the corn mixture to a silky-smooth purée in a food processor. Return the creamed corn to the cleaned saucepan and keep warm.

Sear the scallops on a hot, lightly oiled chargrill plate or non-stick frying pan for 20 seconds on each side and season to taste.

To serve, place some of the creamed corn in the centre of each plate, with the seaweed or spinach in the middle, then arrange three scallops on top, and garnish with three basil leaves. Drizzle with a little shellfish oil, if using.

Serves 6

wine
This dish is quite rich, so the accompanying wine should be reasonably full-bodied. I would be looking at any of the fantastic chardonnays from Margaret River, which is my favourite region for this ubiquitous grape variety. In general, these wines are very intense, with flavours of vanilla, grapefruit, melons and grilled hazelnuts. Pierro, Leeuwin Estate and Moss Wood are all fine examples.

Salad of King Prawns, Crab Cakes and Gremolata

a little olive oil
12 raw king prawns, peeled and deveined, with tails intact
aïoli (see page 206) and gremolata (see page 208), to serve
60 g punnet mâché (lamb's lettuce)
1 preserved lemon (see page 210), rind only, cut into long
    thin strips
1 red onion, finely sliced

Crab cakes
50 g salt
2 thyme sprigs
1 bay leaf
1 rosemary sprig
3 cloves garlic, crushed
150 g blue-eye trevalla fillet, skin removed and pin-boned

150 ml cream
250 ml milk
1 tablespoon grated parmesan
1 teaspoon strained lemon juice
2 tablespoons olive oil
1 tablespoon truffle oil
100 g mashed potato (see page 208)
30 g butter
100 g cooked, picked blue swimmer crab meat
2 eggs, lightly beaten
200 g plain flour
salt and pepper
300 g dried breadcrumbs
vegetable oil, for deep-frying

I love the simplicity of cooking large king prawns – my favourites are the Yamba king prawns from northern New South Wales. Just remember to remove the vein that runs along their backs, otherwise the prawns will be gritty and unappetising. The combination of fried crab cakes, sautéed king prawns and a lemony dressing combined with a rich mayonnaise make this dish a real crowd-pleaser.

For the crab cakes, combine the salt, thyme, bay leaf, rosemary and garlic in a bowl. Place the fish on a large plate, cover with the salt mixture and leave for 1 hour in the fridge. Rinse the fish under cold running water and pat dry with kitchen paper. Place the cream and 150 ml of the milk in a saucepan and bring to the boil, then add the fish and poach, uncovered, for 3–4 minutes, then drain the fish, reserving the liquid. Place the fish, parmesan, lemon juice, olive oil, truffle oil, mashed potato and butter in a bowl and mix together, using a fork to break the fish into flakes; the mixture should be quite moist. Stir through the crab meat then, taking 2 tablespoons of the mixture at a time, mould into round cakes – you should have 12. Place the crab cakes on a baking tray and freeze for about half an hour, to make them easier to crumb.

Combine the eggs and the remaining 100 ml milk in a bowl. Season the flour lightly with salt and pepper, then sift through a fine sieve onto a large plate. Place the breadcrumbs on another large plate. Working one at a time, coat the frozen crab cakes with the flour, shaking off any excess. Coat with the egg and milk mixture, again shaking off any excess, and then roll in the breadcrumbs. Repeat until all the crab cakes are coated and crumbed.

Deep-fry the crab cakes in vegetable oil heated to 200°C in a deep-fryer or heavy-based saucepan for 2–3 minutes or until golden, then remove and drain on kitchen paper.

Heat a little olive oil in a frying pan, add the prawns and pan-fry for 2–3 minutes or until just cooked through.

To serve, place a spoonful of aïoli in the middle of each plate, then place two crab cakes on top, and finish with two prawns. Spoon small dabs of gremolata around the plate, then garnish with mâché, preserved lemon and red onion.

Serves 6

wine
I think one of the richer semillon–sauvignon blanc blends, with flavours of lemon, tropical fruits and a creamy texture, would be ideal with this dish. I would look toward the Yarra Valley in Victoria or the Bordeaux region of France for more savoury examples of this wine.

Chargrilled Lobster with Café de Paris Butter

2 × 800 g live lobsters
a little olive oil
salt and pepper
lemon halves, to serve

Café de Paris butter
250 ml white wine
¼ bunch basil
¼ bunch thyme
¼ bunch chervil
¼ bunch tarragon
½ cup finely chopped flat-leaf parsley
2 cloves garlic, finely chopped
½ cup cornichons, finely chopped

½ cup salted capers, rinsed and finely chopped
12 anchovy fillets, finely chopped
6 golden shallots, finely chopped
750 g butter, softened
finely grated zest and strained juice of 2 lemons
finely grated zest and strained juice of 2 navel oranges
1 tablespoon sweet paprika
1 tablespoon curry powder
60 ml Pernod
80 ml brandy
100 g Dijon mustard
125 ml tomato sauce
100 ml Worcestershire sauce
12 egg yolks

Good-quality lobsters are not cheap; a cheap lobster will be tough and bland to eat and will only have a small amount of meat in it. Try to find southern rock lobsters, sourced from the cold waters of Tasmania. Their meat is tender, sweet and delicious – everything you would expect from this prized crustacean. If you are feeling confident, I recommend you buy live lobsters and plunge them into boiling water. If you are concerned about the lobsters' painful ending, you can always put it into the freezer for an hour to stun it; the lobsters will also be a lot easier to handle this way. After you have cooked the lobsters and allowed them to cool, slice the tails into medallions with the shell still on – this will protect the delicate meat on the barbecue and help to keep it moist. Most importantly, make sure your barbecue is sizzling hot before you grill the lobster medallions, otherwise they will stick. Café de Paris butter is quite time-consuming to make, so it's worth making up a large batch: it keeps well in the freezer for 2–3 months and is perfect on a chargrilled steak or tucked under the skin of a roast chicken. For extra richness, a dozen egg yolks are emulsified in the butter, but the leftover egg whites can be used to make meringues, or frozen for later use.

To make the Café de Paris butter, place the wine, basil, thyme, chervil and tarragon in a saucepan and bring to the boil, then reduce the heat and simmer for 5 minutes or until the liquid reduces to about 2 tablespoons and has a syrupy consistency. Leave to cool, then strain through a sieve placed over a bowl. Add the parsley, garlic, cornichons, capers, anchovies and golden shallots to the wine reduction and stir to combine. Place the softened butter in another bowl and, using a spatula, fold in the wine mixture, lemon and orange zest and juice, paprika and curry powder. Stir in the Pernod, brandy, mustard, tomato ketchup and Worcestershire sauce, then add the egg yolks one at a time, beating well after each addition. Divide the mixture into five equal portions and roll into logs. Wrap each log in plastic film and refrigerate until firm.

Place the lobsters in a large saucepan of boiling salted water and cook for 6 minutes. Turn off the heat but leave the lobsters in the pan for 4 minutes, then drain and refresh in a bowl of iced water. Using a large, heavy knife, such as a chef's knife or a cleaver, cut the lobsters through the shell into 2 cm slices. Chargrill the lobster medallions on a hot, lightly oiled barbecue or chargrill for 2–3 minutes on each side, then season to taste. Thinly slice one of the logs of Café de Paris butter, place a slice on each hot lobster medallion to melt, then serve immediately, with lemon halves to the side.

Serves 4

wine
Forget the wine – this close to chucking a shrimp on the barbie, there is only one drink suggestion: your favourite beer, served icy cold.

Pan-seared Ocean Trout with Hummus, Roasted Peppers, Cumin and Lemon

a little olive oil
6 × 180 g ocean trout fillets, skin-off, pin-boned
6 medium-sized Swiss brown mushrooms, cut into quarters
50 g butter
juice of ½ lemon, strained
salt and pepper

Hummus
200 g dried chickpeas, soaked overnight in cold water
1 litre chicken stock (see page 207)
4 cloves garlic, peeled
2 thyme sprigs
1 teaspoon cumin seeds
1 tablespoon tahini paste
juice of 2 lemons, strained
200 ml extra virgin olive oil

Roasted peppers
3 red peppers
a little olive oil
100 ml honey
1 thyme sprig
2 cloves garlic, crushed
50 ml sherry vinegar

Preserved lemon dressing
2 preserved lemons (see page 210)
250 ml olive oil
125 ml strained lemon juice
¼ bunch flat-leaf parsley, leaves picked

I love ocean trout: it has a high fat content and, as a result, has more flavour and tends to stay moist during cooking. The most time-consuming step of this recipe is the hummus, but you can easily buy a good-quality one from a delicatessen. This dish is equally delicious served cold as part of a buffet.

To make the hummus, drain the chickpeas and place in a large saucepan, along with the chicken stock, garlic and thyme. Bring to the boil, then reduce the heat and simmer for 45–60 minutes or until tender. Meanwhile, dry-roast the cumin seeds in a hot frying pan for about 1 minute, then grind to a powder using a pestle and mortar. Strain the chickpeas through a sieve placed over a bowl, keeping their cooking liquid, but discarding the garlic and herbs. Place the chickpeas and half of the reserved cooking liquid in a food processor and blend until smooth. Add the tahini, ground cumin, lemon juice and olive oil, season to taste and mix well.

For the roasted peppers, blacken the red peppers over a naked flame or under a very hot grill, then place in a bowl and cover with plastic film for 10 minutes. Peel off and discard the blackened skin, then cut each pepper in half, remove the seeds and cut the flesh into thin strips. Transfer to a bowl with a little olive oil and toss to coat, then place on a hot chargrill plate and sear for 1–2 minutes. Place the honey, thyme and garlic in a small saucepan and boil for 1 minute, then add the vinegar to deglaze the pan. Add the chargrilled pepper strips and gently stir through the honey mixture.

For the preserved lemon dressing, cut the preserved lemons into quarters and remove the rind, discarding the flesh. Slice the rind into thin strips, then combine in a bowl with the olive oil and lemon juice and season to taste.

Preheat the oven to 180°C. Heat a little olive oil in an ovenproof frying pan until hot, then cook the fish for 1–2 minutes or until golden. Add the mushrooms to the pan with the fish, then transfer to the oven and bake for 3–4 minutes. Remove the pan from the oven, add the butter and lemon juice to the pan, then turn the fish over and baste with the pan juices.

To serve, spoon some hummus onto each plate and place the mushrooms on top. Arrange strips of roasted pepper over the mushrooms, then top with a piece of fish. Stir the parsley through the preserved lemon dressing, then spoon the dressing over the fish.

Serves 6

Wine
A medium-bodied red wine, such as a South Australian grenache shiraz mataro or a plummy and spicy red wine from the Côtes du Rhône, is good to drink with this dish. The ocean trout is rich enough in texture and flavour to cope with the astringency of these reds.

Pan-fried Salmon Fillet with Poached Egg, Crispy Bacon and Chive Butter Sauce

3 tablespoons olive oil
12 slices bacon
6 × 180 g salmon fillet
salt
100 g butter
juice of 1 lemon, strained
1 bunch spinach
6 teaspoons salmon roe

Poached eggs
2 tablespoons white wine vinegar
6 fresh eggs

Chive butter sauce
100 ml white wine vinegar
10 white peppercorns
100 ml white wine
1 thyme sprig
10 ml cream
250 g unsalted butter, diced
salt and pepper
2 tablespoons finely chopped chives

This makes a great brunch dish – you certainly won't be eating lunch soon afterwards! The sauce is a classic butter sauce or beurre blanc, which is made using a reduction of white wine as a foundation: the acidity from a squeeze of lemon juice added just before serving helps to cut the richness of the bacon and egg.

To poach the eggs, fill a deep frying pan or large saucepan with water and add the vinegar. Bring to the boil then reduce to a simmer until bubbles can just be seen rising. Break each egg into a cup, stir the water with a spoon to create a whirlpool then gently pour in the egg. Cook for 2–3 minutes or until just set, then remove and refresh in bowl of iced water. Repeat with the rest of the eggs.

Make the chive butter sauce by placing the vinegar, peppercorns, white wine and thyme in a small saucepan and reducing over high heat to about 50 ml liquid. Remove the thyme sprig, add the cream and bring to the boil. Reduce the heat to low and whisk in the butter until the sauce is smooth and emulsified. Season to taste and keep warm.

Preheat the oven to 180°C. Heat 1 tablespoon of the olive oil in an ovenproof frying pan, then fry the bacon until crisp. Wipe out the pan with kitchen paper, then add the remaining olive oil and heat. Season the salmon with salt and pan-fry, skin-side down, until the skin is crisp and golden. Transfer the pan to the oven and bake the salmon for 3–4 minutes. Remove

the pan from the oven and turn the salmon over. Place the pan over medium heat on the stovetop, add half the butter and half the lemon juice and baste the fish with the pan juices.

Melt the rest of the butter in another frying pan over low heat and add the spinach. Cook, stirring, for 2 minutes, or until just wilted, then remove from heat and season to taste.

Reheat the poached eggs in boiling water for 1–2 minutes until warmed through. Add the chopped chives and the remaining lemon juice to the sauce and stir through.

To serve, place a salmon fillet on each plate, skin-side up, then place a spoonful of spinach alongside and top with two slices of bacon. Carefully place a poached egg on top of the salmon, then drizzle with chive butter sauce and finish with a teaspoonful of roe.

Serves 6

wine
To my mind, a sparkling or still rosé wine would sit well with this dish. These wines have a focused flavour spectrum of stewed strawberries, redcurrants and plums. A rosé based on either grenache or pinot noir from Geelong or the Mornington Peninsula is highly recommended.

Garfish and Prawn Rolls with Mushrooms, Lime and Muscatels

6 garfish, cleaned and butterflied
a little olive oil
3 large Swiss brown mushrooms, stalks discarded
salt and pepper
175 g salted butter
120 g spinach
60 g seedless dried muscatels
3 limes, peeled and cut into segments with all pith removed

Prawn mousse
80 g raw prawn meat
1 egg white
salt and pepper
40 ml cream
1 tablespoon chopped tarragon

The best garfish is from South Australia, but if you can't find garfish, then small sand whiting are excellent as well. Ask your fishmonger to butterfly the fish for you, and be careful not to overcook the fillets; a few minutes is all they need. This dish has a fragrant, sweet and sour quality to it, thanks to the muscatels and the fresh lime juice.

First, make the prawn mousse. Place the prawn meat in a food processor and process until smooth. Add the egg white, season with salt and pepper and blend, then add the cream and blend again until just combined. Transfer the prawn mixture to a bowl and fold through the chopped tarragon.

Lay out the garfish fillets, skin-side down, on a work bench and spread the prawn mousse evenly over them. Roll up each fillet towards the tail, securing with a toothpick.

Preheat the oven to 180°C. Steam the garfish and prawn rolls in a covered steamer over boiling water for 4–5 minutes. Meanwhile, heat a little olive oil in an ovenproof frying pan, then add the whole mushrooms and season to taste. Transfer to the oven for 2–3 minutes or until tender, then remove from the frying pan and cut in half. Heat a little of the butter in a frying pan, then add the spinach and sauté for 20–30 seconds or until just wilted.

Remove the garfish and prawn rolls from the steamer. Place the spinach in a serving dish and then place the garfish rolls on top, alternating them with the mushroom halves; remove the toothpicks from the garfish rolls. Heat the remaining butter in a hot frying pan until golden and sizzling, then add the muscatels and lime segments. Cook for 30 seconds, then remove from the heat and spoon over the garfish and mushrooms. Serve immediately.

Serves 6

wine
Look for rieslings from the Mount Barker or Great Southern wine regions of Western Australia. These have vibrant flavours of lime zest, minerals and herbs that echo the tastes in this dish.

Pan-fried John Dory with Crushed Kipfler Potatoes and Tomato and Leek Sauce

300 g kipfler potatoes
80 g crème fraîche
125 g double-peeled broad beans, from 500 g beans in pods
salt and pepper
2 tablespoons olive oil
6 × 180 g John Dory fillets, skin-on
25 g butter
juice of ½ lemon, strained
chervil sprigs and extra virgin olive oil, to serve

Tomato and leek sauce
12 large egg tomatoes
50 ml extra virgin olive oil
½ leek, white part only, well-washed and finely chopped
1 clove garlic, finely chopped
salt and pepper

John Dory is a superb eating fish. It is important to make sure the skin has the tell-tale blue mark (or the thumbprint of St Pierre, as it is known); without this, you could be buying silver or mirror dory. Again, as with all thin fish fillets, be careful not to overcook: place the fish, skin-side down, into a hot pan to achieve a golden, crisp skin. To me, the appeal of this dish is that it is simple to prepare and it has a rustic integrity.

First, make the tomato and leek sauce. Remove the tomato stalks and score a cross in the opposite ends. Place in a saucepan of boiling water for 15–20 seconds, then remove and, under cold running water, peel the skin off with your fingers. Cut the tomatoes into quarters, remove the seeds, then cut into small dice. Heat the olive oil in a saucepan, add the leek and garlic and sauté for 2–3 minutes or until translucent. Add the diced tomatoes and season to taste with salt and pepper, then simmer for 10–15 minutes or until the sauce thickens.

Place the potatoes in a saucepan of cold water and bring to the boil, then simmer for 10–15 minutes or until tender. Strain, allow to cool slightly, peel and then crush in a bowl with the back of a fork until chunky. Fold in the crème fraîche. Blanch the broad beans in boiling water for 15–20 seconds, then strain. Add the broad beans to the potatoes and season to taste with salt and pepper.

Heat the olive oil in a frying pan until hot, then pan-fry the John Dory, skin-side down, for 2–3 minutes or until the skin is crisp and golden. Turn over and cook for another 1–2 minutes. Add the butter and lemon juice then baste the fish with the pan juices and remove from the heat.

To serve, place a spoonful of tomato and leek sauce in the centre of each plate. Place the crushed kipfler potatoes on top of the sauce. Top with John Dory fillets, garnish with chervil and finally, drizzle some extra virgin olive oil around the plate.

Serves 6

wine
Give me a glass of Hunter Valley semillon with this dish, and I am a happy man. These wines are very dry and crisp, with an intense flavour of lemons and a whiff of lanolin.

Blue-eye Trevalla with White Bean Purée, Tomatoes, Hazelnuts and Beans

a little olive oil
1 kg blue-eye trevalla fillets, skin-off, pin boned
½ lemon

White bean purée
150 g dried haricot beans, soaked overnight in cold water
½ carrot, peeled and coarsely chopped
1 onion, coarsely chopped
½ celery stalk, coarsely chopped
2 cloves garlic, crushed
2 sprigs thyme
1 bay leaf
1.5 litres chicken stock
100 ml cream
salt and pepper

White bean salad
50 ml olive oil
60 g bacon, cut into strips
60 g hazelnuts
60 g broad beans, from 175 g beans in pods
3 egg tomatoes
60 g baby green beans
180 g cooked white beans, reserved from white bean purée
¼ bunch chives, finely chopped
6 baby watercress sprigs
salt and pepper

I love the meaty texture of this fish. Because of its inherent richness, I like to combine it with equally rich and robust flavours, however if you want a lighter-tasting dish free of meat or poultry flavours, you can always omit the bacon lardons from the salad and substitute the chicken stock used in the white bean purée with water or vegetable stock. The salad has a lovely crunch from the roasted hazelnuts, and the dressing marries the other ingredients together seamlessly. I always like to make a little extra white bean purée to keep in the fridge, ready for spreading on toasted crostini; topped with a drizzle of olive oil, some chopped mint and crushed olives, it makes a great snack. Finally, remember that any red wine sauce will only be as good as the red wine you put in it!

To make the white bean purée, drain the soaked beans, then rinse under cold running water. Place the beans, carrot, onion, celery, garlic, thyme, bay leaf and chicken stock in a large saucepan. Bring to the boil, then reduce the heat and simmer for 1 hour or until the beans are tender. Strain the bean mixture, removing and discarding the vegetables. Reserve 180 g of the white beans for the white bean salad, then purée the rest in a food processor while they are still hot. Bring the cream to the boil in a small saucepan then add to the beans in the processor, and process until smooth. Season with salt and pepper to taste.

Next, make the white bean salad. Preheat the oven to 180°C. Heat the olive oil in a frying pan and pan-fry the bacon lardons until crisp then drain on kitchen paper. Spread the hazelnuts on a baking tray and roast in the oven for 2–3 minutes; remove the hazelnuts but leave the oven on, ready for the fish. Blanch the broad beans in a saucepan of boiling water for 30–40 seconds and refresh under cold running water, then double-peel them by removing their outer skin. Score both ends of the egg tomatoes with a sharp knife and place in a bowl of boiling water for 2–3 minutes, then refresh under cold running water. Peel the tomatoes with your fingers, then deseed and cut into dice. Blanch the baby green beans in a saucepan of boiling salted water for 1–2 minutes and refresh under cold running water. Combine the reserved white beans with the lardons, hazelnuts, broad beans, tomatoes, green beans, chives and watercress in a bowl and season to taste. >

Hazelnut dressing
1 teaspoon Dijon mustard
25 ml chardonnay vinegar
55 ml honey
½ clove garlic, crushed
110 ml hazelnut oil
salt and pepper

Red wine sauce
1 golden shallot, thinly sliced
250 ml red wine
50 g castor sugar
25 ml red wine vinegar
1 tablespoon cream
100 g cultured unsalted butter, diced

For the hazelnut dressing, combine the mustard, vinegar, honey and garlic in small bowl. Slowly whisk in the oil until all the ingredients are emulsified, then season to taste.

To make the red wine sauce, place the golden shallots, red wine, sugar and vinegar in a small saucepan over high heat and cook for about 10 minutes, or until the liquid is reduced by a quarter and has a syrupy consistency. Add the cream and bring back to the boil. Remove from the heat and gradually add the butter, whisking to emulsify. Keep warm.

Cut the blue-eye trevalla into 18 slices, each about 1 cm thick. Heat a little olive oil in an ovenproof frying pan until hot, then pan-fry the trevalla slices for 1–2 minutes or until golden. Transfer to the oven and cook for 1–2 minutes. Remove the pan from the oven, turn the trevalla slices over, add a squeeze of lemon juice and baste the fish with the pan juices.

When ready to serve, reheat the white bean purée and gently toss the white bean salad with the hazelnut dressing. Place a small amount of the warm white bean purée in the centre of each plate, with a spoonful of white bean salad on top. Arrange three pieces of fish on each plate, then drizzle a little red wine sauce around the plate.

Serves 6

wine

Perhaps a delicate cool-climate shiraz from Victoria would work well with this dish – these wines can be fragrant and spicy, but won't overpower the fish at all.

Crumbed King George Whiting and Sauce Gribiche

2 eggs
100 ml milk
100 g plain flour
200 g Japanese breadcrumbs
12 King George whiting fillets, skin-off,
    pin-boned and cut in half lengthways
3 lemons, cut into halves
50 ml grapeseed or vegetable oil
10 g butter

Sauce gribiche
2 eggs
50 g gherkin, finely chopped
50 g capers, finely chopped
80 ml mayonnaise (see page 209)
30 g chervil, finely chopped
30 g tarragon, finely chopped

King George whiting is a wonderful Australian fish, with a delicate texture but an intense flavour. Japanese breadcrumbs are available from speciality Asian food stores. I prefer them as they are finer, but regular dried breadcrumbs can be used if necessary. It is important to make sure that your oil is both hot and fresh, as you don't want the fish to take on the flavour of stale oil. I like to use a neutral-tasting oil, such as grapeseed or vegetable oil. Sauce gribiche is a variation on the traditional tartare sauce, and of course you must have plenty of lemon wedges on hand.

To make the sauce gribiche, hard-boil the eggs for 7–8 minutes, then shell them and separate the whites from the yolks. Roughly chop the whites (keep the yolks for a sandwich), then transfer to a bowl. Add the gherkin, capers, mayonnaise, chervil and tarragon and stir to combine. Cover with plastic film and refrigerate.

For the fish, lightly whisk the eggs and milk together in a bowl. Sift the flour onto a large plate, and scatter the Japanese breadcrumbs over another large plate. Pass the whiting fillets through the flour, dusting off the excess, then dip them into the egg and milk mixture before coating in the breadcrumbs. Heat the oil and butter in a large frying pan until hot, then pan-fry the fish for 2–3 minutes on each side until golden brown. When the fish is cooked, place on kitchen paper to absorb any excess oil.

Allow four pieces of fish per person, and serve with sauce gribiche and a lemon half alongside.

Serves 6

wine
Fish and chips always remind me of holidays and hot summer evenings at a beach house. A chilled bottle of New Zealand sauvignon blanc is the obvious wine choice here, a refreshing white with flavours of ripe pineapple and mangoes, and a crisp dry finish. Yum!

Crisp-skinned Snapper with Chat Potatoes, Baby Beetroot and a Tarragon Salsa

rock salt
18 cherry tomatoes
300 ml pickling mix (see page 209)
9 baby beetroot
9 chat potatoes
18 pearl onions, trimmed
100 g butter
a little olive oil
salt and pepper
12 × 100 g baby snapper fillets *or*
     6 × 180 g snapper fillets, skin-on, pin-boned
juice of ½ lemon, strained
tarragon sprigs, to serve

Tarragon salsa
1 slice white bread, crust removed
a little milk
2 bunches tarragon, leaves picked
1 clove garlic, crushed
100 ml olive oil
50 ml chardonnay vinegar

This is a great, rustic, Italian-inspired fish dish. The pickled beetroot will keep for months and can also be served in salads, or as a condiment with game or meat terrines or pâtés. The tarragon salsa adds freshness and piquancy to the dish, bringing its flavours to life; any leftover salsa makes a great addition to offal dishes, such as lamb's brains, liver or kidneys.

Preheat the oven to 100°C. Cover the base of a roasting tin with rock salt, place the cherry tomatoes on top and roast for 2 hours. Remove and leave to cool. Increase the oven temperature to 200°C.

To make the tarragon salsa, place the bread in a shallow bowl and cover with a little milk to soften. Leave for about 2 minutes, then squeeze out any excess liquid with your hands. Place the bread, tarragon, garlic and olive oil in a food processor and blend for approximately 1 minute or until smooth. Blend in the vinegar just before serving, otherwise the salsa will discolour.

Place the pickling mix in a saucepan and bring to the boil, then add the beetroot and simmer for about 15 minutes, or until tender. Remove from the heat and leave the beetroot to cool in the liquid. Drain the beetroot and peel with your fingers (use disposable gloves if you want to avoid stained hands!), cut each baby beetroot in half and set aside.

Place the chat potatoes in a saucepan of cold water and bring to the boil, then simmer for 10–15 minutes or until tender. Drain and cut in half, then set aside. Blanch the pearl onions in boiling salted water for 3–4 minutes or until tender, then drain. Place 50 g butter and a little oil in a saucepan and heat until the butter melts, then add the pearl onions and cook for 3 minutes or until caramelised and golden. Season with salt and pepper to taste.

Heat a little olive oil in an ovenproof frying pan until hot, then add the snapper fillets, skin-side down. Using a spatula, apply light pressure to the top of the fillets to stop the skin from shrinking too much. Cook for 1–2 minutes or until golden, then transfer to the oven and bake for 4–5 minutes. Remove the pan from the oven, turn the snapper fillets over and add the lemon juice and remaining butter. Baste the fish with the pan juices, then remove from the pan.

To serve, divide the tomatoes, beetroot, chat potatoes and onions among six plates. Drizzle over the tarragon salsa, scatter with some tarragon sprigs and arrange the fish alongside.

Serves 6

wine
Gavi is a delicious dry Italian white wine that hails from the Piedmont region of north-east Italy. Made from the cortese grape, it is best drunk young. Gavi is light, spritzy and lively, with peach, citrus, vanilla and mineral flavours.

Jewfish with Mushroom Crust and Gremolata

Mushroom crust
40 g cultured unsalted butter
5 golden shallots, finely chopped
1 clove garlic, finely chopped
2 thyme sprigs
1 bay leaf
400 g button mushrooms, sliced
50 g porcini mushrooms, diced
2 tablespoons truffle oil – optional
salt and pepper

Fennel cream
25 g cultured unsalted butter
2 medium-sized baby fennel bulbs, trimmed and thinly sliced
salt
100 ml chicken stock
80 g fromage frais

This is a great fish dish to serve in autumn. I like to use the farmed jewfish from the Spencer Gulf in South Australia, which is marketed as Suzuki mulloway. The aquaculture behind the development of this particular fish means that its size, availability, price and, most importantly, flavour are of a consistently high standard. If you cannot find the Suzuki mulloway jewfish, regular wild jewfish will suffice. This fish recipe is perfect for a dinner party, since it requires literally only 2 minutes in the kitchen away from your guests: the fish can be seared and topped with the mushroom and truffle crust in advance, then refrigerated. When you're ready to eat, all you need do is flash the fish in the oven and quickly brown it under the grill before serving. In the recipe below, the potatoes are served as a warm salad with the fennel cream, but for a simpler dish, just serve the fish with pan-fried or crunchy roast potatoes. Porcini mushrooms are available frozen or dried from specialist food shops. If using dried porcini, soak in a little warm water first. The truffle oil is, of course, an optional indulgence.

For the mushroom crust, melt the butter in a frying pan and pan-fry the shallots, garlic, thyme and bay leaf for 2–3 minutes or until the shallots are translucent; do not allow to brown. Add the button and porcini mushrooms to the frying pan and cook over high heat, stirring constantly, until all the moisture from the mushrooms has evaporated – this may take up to 20 minutes. Add the truffle oil, if using, and season to taste with salt and pepper. Transfer to a food processor and process to a rustic, finely chopped consistency; do not purée. Line a baking tray with baking paper and spread with a 5 mm layer of the mushroom mixture, then cover with another sheet of baking paper and place in the freezer for approximately 30 minutes or until frozen. Remove from the freezer and cut into six rectangles to fit on top of the jewfish fillets, then return to the freezer until ready to proceed.

For the fennel cream, melt the butter in a small saucepan, add the fennel and season with salt (this will help to draw the moisture from the fennel). Cook for 3–4 minutes or until translucent; do not allow to brown. Add the chicken stock and simmer, covered, for approximately 10–15 minutes or until very tender. Purée the cooked fennel using a hand-held blender, then pass through a sieve placed over a bowl and leave to cool. Fold in the fromage frais and adjust the seasoning if necessary. >

9 medium-sized kipfler potatoes
a little olive oil
6 × 160 g Suzuki mulloway jewfish fillets,
    skin-off, pin-boned
120 g dried breadcrumbs
1 bunch baby cress, leaves picked
¼ bunch dill, leaves picked
¼ bunch flat-leaf parsley, leaves picked
1 quantity gremolata (see page 208)

Place the potatoes in a saucepan, then add just enough
cold water to cover and a little salt, if desired. Bring to the boil
and cook for approximately 10–15 minutes or until tender,
then drain. When the potatoes are cool enough to handle,
carefully peel off the skins with your fingers, then cut each
potato into 5 mm slices.

Preheat the oven to 180°C, and the grill to high. Heat
the olive oil in an ovenproof frying pan over high heat, then
sear the jewfish fillets on each side for 1–2 minutes. Place the
chilled mushroom crust on top of the jewfish fillets, transfer
the pan to the oven and bake for 3–4 minutes. Remove the
fish from the oven, sprinkle the breadcrumbs on top and place
under the grill for less than a minute, until golden brown.

To serve, arrange five or six potato slices on each plate,
then place three spoonfuls of fennel cream around them.
Gently toss together the baby cress, dill and parsley then place
on top of the potatoes. Finish the gremolata by mixing in the
lemon juice, then drizzle over the top of the herbs. Place the
baked fish on top and serve immediately.

Serves 6

Wine
*I would recommend a savoury, medium-bodied white wine, such
as a marsanne, with this robust fish dish. Wines made from this
grape variety have a rich, honeyed texture, underpinned with
notes of roasted nuts and tobacco.*

Pesto-crusted Barramundi with Fondant Potatoes and Roast Tomato Sauce

a little olive oil
6 × 180 g barramundi fillets, skin-off, pin-boned
25 g butter
250 g shimeji mushrooms
salt and pepper
6 chervil sprigs

Pesto crust
2 tablespoons pesto (see page 209)
20 g parmesan, grated
160 g brioche crumbs
30 g gruyère
80 g butter
1 bunch flat-leaf parsley, leaves picked and finely chopped
finely grated zest of ½ lemon

Roast tomato sauce
500 g egg tomatoes, halved
50 ml olive oil
2 cloves garlic, crushed
5 thyme sprigs, leaves picked and coarsely chopped
salt and pepper

Fondant potatoes
250 g salted butter, softened
6 desiree potatoes
salt

This is my favourite Mediterranean-style fish dish. When making the pesto, use the freshest herbs, to obtain a vibrant green colour.

For the pesto crust, place all the ingredients in a food processor and blend until the mixture becomes a green dough. Place the dough between two sheets of baking paper and roll out to 4 mm thick. Wrap in plastic film and freeze until ready to use.

To make the fondant potatoes, spread the butter over the base of a large saucepan. Peel and cut each potato into a 6 × 3 cm cylinder and place on top of the butter. The potatoes should fit snugly into the saucepan but they must not touch each other. Season with salt and pour in just enough water to cover the potatoes. Cut a circle of baking paper to fit the pan, butter it and place it on top of the potatoes. Bring to the boil, then reduce heat and simmer until all the water and butter has been absorbed and the potatoes have caramelised – this should take about 30–40 minutes. Don't shake the pan while the potatoes are cooking, as this will affect the caramelisation. Check if they are cooked by inserting a skewer through the centre; it may be necessary to add more water so that the butter does not burn. Remove from the heat and leave to cool, then carefully transfer each potato cylinder to a baking tray. Set aside.

For the roast tomato sauce, preheat the oven to 180°C. Place the halved tomatoes, oil, garlic and thyme in a bowl and toss to combine. Transfer to a baking tray, season with salt and pepper and roast for 20 minutes or until the tomatoes are very soft. Purée the tomatoes in a food processor then pass through a fine sieve placed over a small saucepan; use the back of a spoon to press as much as possible through the sieve, as the thickness of the sauce will depend on it. Season with salt and pepper to taste then set aside.

Heat a little olive oil in an ovenproof frying pan until hot, and pan-fry the barramundi for 1–2 minutes on each side or until golden, then transfer to the oven and bake for 5–6 minutes. Preheat the grill to medium. Remove the fish from the oven, then place the potatoes in the oven to reheat for about 5 minutes. Meanwhile, take the pesto crust from the freezer and cut it into six rectangles to fit on top of the barramundi fillets. Place the pesto-topped fish under the grill for 2 minutes; do not allow the crust to brown, just to warm through.

Melt the 25 g of butter in a hot frying pan and pan-fry the mushrooms for 1–2 minutes, then season to taste. Gently warm the roast tomato sauce (do not boil), then spoon a little in the centre of each plate. Place a fondant potato to one side and top with mushrooms and a sprig of chervil. Place the barramundi on the other side and serve immediately.

Serves 6

wine
There are some beautiful white viogniers being produced in Australia nowadays. These wines are rich, with heady apricot and floral flavours, and quite viscous in texture, but they have a good acid balance that is tremendous with this dish.

POULTRY & GAME

Pressed Rabbit Terrine with Cornichons

3 × 1.5 kg farmed rabbits, cut into legs, shoulders and loins
200 g salt
5 rosemary sprigs, leaves picked
5 thyme sprigs, leaves picked
7 cloves garlic, crushed
1 kg duck fat *or* 1 litre olive oil
salt and pepper

100 ml sherry vinegar
120 g bacon, thinly sliced
70 g butter
200 ml chicken stock
1½ gelatine leaves, softened in cold water
crusty bread and cornichons, to serve

This rabbit terrine is easier than it looks. Ask your butcher to clean and prepare the rabbits, separating them into legs, shoulders and loins (and keeping the kidney, liver and fillet), then do all the preparation the day before and refrigerate overnight. Let the terrine come to room temperature before eating: I like to serve it in the traditional French way with baby cornichons and crusty bread, but you could also try it with fig jam, pickled quinces or pear chutney. The terrine can be made using duck instead of rabbit, if you prefer.

Set aside the rabbit loins, fillets, kidney and liver. Place the rabbit legs and shoulders in a large bowl. Mix together the salt, rosemary, thyme and garlic, then rub this over the rabbit legs and shoulders and leave to marinate for 3–4 hours in the fridge.

Preheat the oven to 150°C. Rinse the rabbit legs and shoulders under cold water, then place in a roasting tin and pour over enough melted duck fat or olive oil to cover. Cook in the oven for 2–3 hours, until the meat is falling off the bones. Strain off the fat and, when the rabbit pieces are cool enough to handle, pick all the meat from the bones, and season with salt, pepper and sherry vinegar. Reserve some nice chunky pieces, then shred the rest of the meat. Set aside.

Line a 30 × 15 cm terrine mould with plastic film, then line the mould with the bacon so that the slices overlap slightly and overhang the edges by about 8 cm. Season the loins, fillets, kidney and liver with salt and pepper. Melt the butter in a frying pan over medium heat, add the loins and cook for 3–4 minutes, then remove. Add the liver and kidney to the same pan and cook for 2 minutes, then remove. Finally, add the fillets to the pan and cook for 30 seconds then remove. (All the pan-fried rabbit should be cooked to medium-rare.)

To assemble the terrine, place enough shredded confit rabbit meat in the mould to cover the base, then add the loins, fillets, kidney, liver and the reserved chunks of confit rabbit meat. Cover with the remaining shredded confit rabbit meat, pressing it down lightly to fill any gaps.

Warm the chicken stock in a small saucepan, then dissolve the gelatine in it and season to taste. Pour the stock over the terrine, then press down to ensure there are no air pockets. Fold the overhanging bacon across the top of the terrine so that it is completely encased, then cover and refrigerate for at least 10 hours; it will keep in the fridge for 5–7 days.

To serve, carefully turn the terrine out of the mould, cut into 1 cm slices and eat with cornichons and crusty bread.

Serves 12–14

wine
This terrine needs a white wine that is medium-bodied, fresh and tart – perhaps a crisp, clean French Chablis or an unwooded chardonnay.

Chicken Breast with Caramelised Peaches and Aged Balsamic

6 chicken breasts off the bone, skin-on
3 peaches
30 g butter
40 g sugar
juice of 1 lemon, strained
60 ml olive oil
1 bunch watercress, picked and washed
30 ml aged balsamic vinegar

Stuffing
30 g butter
½ white onion, finely diced
1 clove garlic, crushed
1 teaspoon chopped thyme
200 g chicken thigh fillets
1 slice pancetta
finely grated zest of ½ orange
1 tablespoon brandy
salt and pepper

This is a great dinner party dish that is twice-cooked, which means you can poach the chicken in advance and refrigerate it, so that all you need to do is sear it and then heat it through in the oven. Caramelised peaches and watercress always remind me of my favourite foie gras dish, which is served with this classic garnish at Quaglino's in London. The balsamic vinegar offsets the caramelised sweetness of the peaches.

To make the stuffing, heat the butter in a frying pan and cook the onion, garlic and thyme for 2–3 minutes, or until the onion is translucent, then allow to cool. Mince the chicken thigh fillets and pancetta in a food processor, then transfer to a bowl and stir through the cooled onion mixture, orange zest and brandy, seasoning with salt and pepper.

Using a paring knife, make a small incision in each chicken breast and pipe in the stuffing (or simply ease the stuffing under the skin with your fingers). Wrap each chicken breast firmly in plastic film, tying each end securely with a knot and making sure there is no air trapped inside. Place the wrapped chicken breasts in a large saucepan of boiling water, reduce the heat and simmer for 10 minutes, then remove and refresh in a large bowl of iced water. Allow to cool, then remove the plastic film and drain on kitchen paper to absorb any excess moisture.

Score a cross in one end of the peaches and blanch in boiling water for 30 seconds, then refresh under cold running water. Remove the skin and stone, and cut each peach into eight wedges. Melt the butter in a saucepan, then add the sugar, stirring over medium heat until a caramel is formed – this will take about 2–3 minutes. Add the peaches and stir to coat with the caramel. Add the lemon juice, then remove from the heat and transfer the peaches to a large plate or bowl to cool.

Preheat the oven to 180°C. Heat half of the olive oil in an ovenproof frying pan and, when hot, sear the chicken breasts for 2–3 minutes, or until golden brown all over. Transfer the pan to the oven for 10 minutes, then remove and allow the chicken to rest for 10 minutes.

Slice each chicken breast into four slices on an angle and arrange on the plate. Place the caramelised peaches alongside, garnish with watercress and drizzle with remaining olive oil and the balsamic vinegar.

Serves 6

Wine
Viognier has varietal flavours of apricots and peaches balanced with a crisp acid finish, which work a treat with this dish.

Roast Breast of Guinea Fowl with Pumpkin and Truffled Peas

6 × 150 g guinea fowl breasts, skin-on
olive oil
90 ml chicken jus (see page 206)
chervil or celery cress sprigs, to serve

Chicken and tarragon mousse
250 g chicken breast fillet, well-chilled
1 egg white, chilled
300 ml cream, chilled
½ bunch tarragon, leaves picked and chopped
salt and pepper

Pumpkin purée
1 kg blue pumpkin, peeled and cut into 1 cm dice
2 cloves garlic, chopped
1 tablespoon olive oil
½ teaspoon Dijon mustard
50 g mustard fruits
50 g butter

Truffled peas
40 g shelled peas, from 80 g peas in pods
1 teaspoon truffle oil
1 teaspoon strained lemon juice

Guinea fowl is not as rich as duck, but definitely has a little more flavour than chicken. The tarragon and chicken mousse adds a lovely herbaceous perfume and the pumpkin purée benefits from the sweet peppery flavour of mustard fruits. This recipe works equally well with chicken breasts.

To make the chicken and tarragon mousse, place the chicken breast in a food processor and process to a fine mince. Add the egg white, process again, and then slowly add the cream and process until combined. Transfer the mousse to a bowl and stir through the tarragon, then season and allow to rest for 30 minutes in the fridge.

Meanwhile, make the pumpkin purée. Preheat the oven to 180° C. Place the pumpkin in a roasting tin with the garlic and olive oil and roast for 20 minutes, or until tender. Remove the pumpkin from the oven, then increase the oven temperature to 200°C. Purée the roast pumpkin in a food processor with the mustard, mustard fruits and butter. Season to taste, then pass through a fine sieve into a saucepan.

Using a paring knife, make a small incision in each guinea fowl breast and pipe in the chicken and tarragon mousse.

Heat a little olive oil in an ovenproof frying pan, add the guinea fowl breasts, skin-side down, and cook until golden, then turn and cook for another 1–2 minutes. Transfer to the oven and cook for a further 8 minutes, then remove from the oven and allow to rest for 10 minutes.

While the guinea fowl is resting, cook the peas in boiling water for 1–2 minutes, strain, then stir through the truffle oil and lemon juice. Gently heat the chicken jus and reheat the pumpkin purée.

To serve, place some pumpkin purée in the middle of each plate with the peas surrounding it. Slice the guinea fowl breasts at an angle and place on top of the purée, then finish with chicken jus and garnish with chervil or celery cress.

Serves 6

wine
I would serve a buttery white burgundy, with dominant flavours of white peach, almonds and butterscotch.

Roast Duck Breast with Cherries

6 × 180 g duck breasts, preferably from Muscovy ducks, skin-on
salt and pepper
1 tablespoon olive oil
40 g butter
2 bunches spinach, trimmed and well-washed

Duck pastia
½ teaspoon ground ginger
1 teaspoon ground white pepper
1 teaspoon ground black pepper
½ teaspoon ground nutmeg
pinch ground cloves
1 tablespoon olive oil
1 onion, sliced
1 thyme sprig

50 ml chicken stock
1 Peking duck breast fillet, diced
1 tablespoon sultanas
½ teaspoon cocoa powder
1 tablespoon brandy
1 × 375 g packet filo pastry
50 g butter, melted

Celeriac purée
20 g butter
200 g celeriac, diced
100 ml milk
100 ml cream
salt and pepper

Duck breast should be served pink, and it is very important to rest the meat after cooking for 10 minutes before you carve it, otherwise it will be tough. In summer I always buy a couple of boxes of cherries and preserve them, so I can eat them all year round, but you could always get preserved or spiced cherries from a good delicatessen.

A pastia is essentially a small pastry with a savoury or sweet filling. Ideally, pastia are made with brik pastry (very fine pastry sheets imported from Tunisia), but filo pastry makes a good substitute. In this recipe, the nutmeg and clove are ideal flavourings for the chopped duck pastia filling.

To make the filling for the duck pastia, combine the ginger, white and black pepper, nutmeg and cloves in a dry frying pan and heat until aromatic, then transfer to a small bowl and set aside. Heat the oil in the frying pan over high heat, add the onion and thyme, and fry for 3–5 minutes until the onion is caramelised. Reduce the heat, then add the chicken stock and simmer for about 5 minutes, or until most of the liquid has evaporated, leaving a moist caramelised onion mixture. Transfer to a bowl and combine with the diced duck

breast, sultanas, cocoa powder, brandy, and ¼ teaspoon of the combined spices (the remaining spice mixture keeps well in the pantry, and can be used to enliven a terrine, fish dishes or fruit cakes). Season with salt.

To assemble the duck pastia, lay a sheet of filo pastry on the bench and brush with melted butter. Place another filo sheet on top, then cut the pastry lengthwise into three pieces and brush with butter again. Put 2 tablespoons of the duck mixture at the end of a sheet of filo and fold over the corner to completely enclose the filling and form a triangle. Keep folding the pastry over, retaining the triangle shape, until you get to the end of the sheet. Repeat with the remaining pastry and filling. Place the pastia on a lightly greased baking tray, brush the tops with butter and place in the refrigerator.

For the celeriac purée, melt the butter in a saucepan over low heat, then add the diced celeriac and cook, covered, for approximately 5 minutes, or until it is just tender. Add the milk and cream and simmer for 5–10 minutes then strain. Purée the celeriac in a food processor, season to taste, then pass through a sieve into a saucepan and keep warm. >

Duck sauce

300 g duck wings, roughly chopped (ask your butcher to do this)
1 tablespoon olive oil
6 golden shallots, finely sliced
1 bay leaf
3 thyme sprigs
2 cloves garlic
60 ml sherry vinegar
500 ml veal jus (see page 211)
20 white peppercorns
30 preserved cherries (see page 210)

Next, make the duck sauce. Preheat the oven to 200°C. Place the duck wings in a roasting tin and roast for 10–15 minutes until golden brown. (Leave the oven on, ready to cook the pastia.) Heat the oil in a frying pan over low–medium heat and gently fry the shallots with the bay leaf, thyme and garlic for 3–4 minutes, without browning. Add the roast duck wings, along with the vinegar and veal jus, then simmer for approximately 20–30 minutes, or until reduced to a sauce consistency. Strain the sauce through a muslin-lined sieve into a saucepan.

Score the skin side of the duck breasts and season with salt and pepper. Heat the oil in a frying pan over medium heat and add the duck breasts, skin-side down. Cook on this side for about 4–6 minutes, or until the skin is crisp and golden, then turn over and cook for a further 3–4 minutes. If the duck breasts are thick, place in the oven for a further 2–3 minutes. Remove from the pan and leave to rest in a warm place for 10 minutes.

While the duck is resting, cook the pastia and the spinach, and finish the duck sauce. Melt 20 g of the butter in a frying pan over medium heat and fry the pastia for 2 minutes on each side, then return to the baking tray and cook in the oven for a further 2 minutes. Melt the remaining 20 g of butter in a saucepan over medium heat, then add the spinach and cook until just wilted, seasoning with salt and pepper to taste. Gently reheat the duck sauce and add the cherries.

To serve, place a pile of spinach on each plate with a little celeriac purée to one side. Slice the duck breasts and arrange on each plate. Lean a pastia against the duck and drizzle the sauce and cherries over.

Serves 6

wine

Duck and pinot noir is one of the great food and wine matches. The choice now is better than ever, but my favourite pinot noirs are from the Martinborough region of New Zealand – these wines are a complex mix of wild berries, smoke, spice and truffle.

Duck and Pea Pie with Pea Purée

2.2 kg duck Marylands, skin-off
salt and pepper
1 tablespoon olive oil
1 carrot, diced
2 celery stalks, diced
1 onion, diced
½ small leek, white part only, well-washed and finely chopped
100 ml Madeira
1 litre chicken stock
½ clove garlic, finely chopped
½ bunch thyme, leaves picked
½ bunch tarragon, leaves picked and chopped
1 whole Chinese roast duck, meat removed from bones and diced

150 g shelled peas, from 300 g peas in pods or 150 g frozen peas
1 bunch spinach
1.25 kg puff pastry
1 egg, lightly beaten

Pea purée
250 g shelled peas, from 500 g peas in pods or 250 g frozen peas
25 g butter
1 medium-sized onion, finely chopped
½ clove garlic, finely chopped
100 ml chicken stock
salt and pepper

I have a real sentimental attachment to this duck dish, which I first started cooking 15 years ago at my first restaurant, The Paddington Inn Bistro. As this recipe makes such fall-apart tender duck meat, it is a good idea to throw in a few extra duck pieces – the cooked duck meat will keep for 2–3 days in the fridge, and is great folded through wide strips of pasta with some peas and grated parmesan.

First, make the filling for the pies. Preheat the oven to 140°C. Season the duck Marylands with salt and pepper. Heat the olive oil in an ovenproof heavy-based pan over high heat and brown the duck on all sides. Remove and set aside, then add the carrot, celery, onion and leek and cook for approximately 5 minutes. Deglaze the pan with the Madeira, scraping the bottom to incorporate all the flavours. Return the duck to the pan, then add the chicken stock, garlic, thyme and tarragon and bring to the boil. Transfer to the oven and braise for 2½ hours until meat is almost falling off the bone. Remove from the oven, then increase the temperature to 200°C, ready for the pies. Take the duck and vegetables from the pan. When cool enough to handle, pull all the duck meat from the bones and set aside, along with the vegetables. Skim excess fat from the braising liquid and reduce until it is a sauce consistency, then pour over the duck and vegetables. Add the roast duck meat and the peas then leave to cool. To blanch the spinach leaves, plunge them into boiling water, immediately drain and run under cold water, then lay the leaves out to dry on a clean tea towel.

Next, assemble the pies. Divide the duck and vegetable mixture into eight equal portions, roll each into a ball, and wrap in the blanched spinach leaves. Cut the puff pastry into eight circles about 8 cm in diameter, and then cut out another eight circles 11 cm in diameter. Place a spinach-wrapped ball of duck in the middle of each smaller pastry circle then lightly brush the edges of the pastry with beaten egg. Cover with the larger pastry circle, pressing the edges to seal. If desired, decorate the pies by using the edge of a fork to create a swirl effect. Place the pies on a greased baking tray and brush with the beaten egg. Bake for 20–25 minutes until golden.

While the pies are cooking, make the pea purée. Blanch the peas in boiling water for 1 minute, then drain and refresh under cold running water. Melt the butter in a saucepan, add the onion and garlic and cook until tender and translucent, without browning. Add the chicken stock and simmer for 3 minutes, then add the peas. Cook the peas for 1–2 minutes or until tender, then transfer the peas with their cooking liquid to a food processor and purée. Season to taste.

To serve, spread a small amount of pea purée in the centre of the plate and place a pie on top, fresh from the oven.

Serves 8

wine
A rich, dark merlot is a good option here – these wines have flavours of plums, tobacco, cedar and a touch of leafiness.

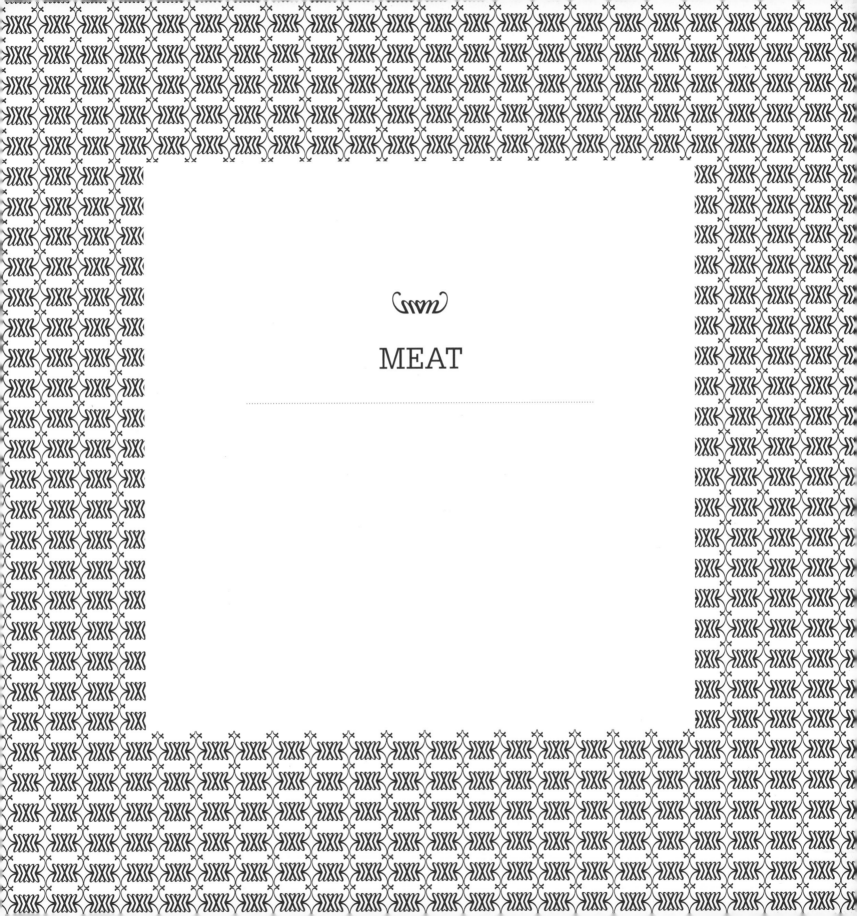

MEAT

Pan-fried Calves' Liver with Prosciutto and Sweet Potato Mash

12 slices prosciutto, cut in half lengthways
1 kg calves' liver, cut into 12 slices (or get your butcher to do this)
salt and pepper
2 tablespoons olive oil
watercress sprigs, to serve

Sweet potato mash
1 kg sweet potato, peeled and diced
1.2 litres chicken stock
salt and pepper
40 g butter
100 g honey
2 cloves garlic, finely chopped

Onion gravy
30 g butter
1 onion, thinly sliced
2 tablespoons sherry vinegar
300 ml veal jus (see page 211)
salt and pepper

This dish is very similar to one that was on my first menu at Paddington Inn Bistro many years ago – that dish used duck livers, but it was served in the same way. I love the combination of the smoky flavour of the crisp prosciutto and the sweetness of the sweet potato purée. It is important that the calves' liver is not sliced too thinly, as it can easily be overcooked.

For the sweet potato mash, place the sweet potato and chicken stock in a large saucepan. Add a pinch of salt, bring to the boil and simmer for 15–20 minutes or until tender. Drain, then purée the sweet potatoes in a food processor, adding the butter, honey and garlic. Season to taste and keep warm.

For the onion gravy, melt the butter in a frying pan and, when hot, add the onion and cook for 3–4 minutes or until it is golden and soft. Add the sherry vinegar to the pan and simmer for 2–3 minutes, or until reduced by half. Pour in the veal jus and simmer for 5 minutes. Season to taste and keep warm.

Wrap two pieces of prosciutto around each piece of liver and season with salt and pepper. Heat the oil in a frying pan until hot, then pan-fry the liver for 2 minutes on each side or until medium-rare.

Place some warm sweet potato mash in the middle of each plate, then put two pieces of liver on top. Spoon over the onion gravy, and garnish with the watercress.

Serves 6

wine

An elegant, softer style of red wine is my recommendation here – perhaps a medium-bodied cabernet sauvignon rich in blackcurrant fruits.

Veal Cutlets with Persillade and Mushrooms

100 g pork caul
juice of 1 lemon
6 thick veal cutlets
salt and pepper
a little olive oil
20 g butter
350 g wild mushrooms, such as chanterelles and
    morels *or* 350 g Swiss brown mushrooms
chervil or flat-leaf parsley sprigs, to serve

Persillade
140 g bone marrow
2 bunches flat-leaf parsley, finely chopped
2 cloves garlic, roughly chopped

Madeira sauce
50 g butter
200 g veal trimmings
1 tablespoon chopped golden shallots
150 g button mushrooms, sliced
2 cloves garlic, chopped
2 thyme sprigs
500 ml Madeira
750 ml veal jus (see page 211)

Making persillade transports me back to 1985, when I worked as a first apprentice at La Belle Helene restaurant on Sydney's north shore. Back in those days, as a 15-year-old kid, I used to turn up my nose up when I had to make persillade. Nowadays, I've matured a bit and I love it! This is a very rustic, bistro-style dish that is great to eat on a cold winter's night, served with mashed potato (see page 208). The pork caul, veal trimmings and bone marrow needed for this recipe should all be available from most butchers, although you may need to order them in advance.

First, prepare the pork caul by soaking it in cold water with a squeeze of lemon juice for about 2 hours, changing the water two or three times.

For the persillade, place the bone marrow, parsley and garlic in a food processor and blend until it becomes a smooth green paste. Roll out into a large log. Wrap the persillade in plastic film and refrigerate for at least 30 minutes until firm.

For the Madeira sauce, melt the butter in a frying pan and sauté the veal trimmings until brown. Add the shallots, mushrooms, garlic and thyme and sauté for another 5 minutes. Pour in the Madeira, stir and simmer for 5–10 minutes or until reduced by half, then add the veal jus. Bring back to the boil, skim any scum from the surface, then reduce the heat and simmer for 30 minutes. Strain the sauce through a muslin-lined sieve placed over a saucepan and keep warm.

Preheat the oven to 180°C. Season each veal cutlet with a little salt and pepper. Heat a little olive oil in a frying pan over high heat and seal the cutlets for 2 minutes on each side, then place on a baking tray and allow to cool. Remove the plastic film from the persillade and cut into 1 cm slices, then place a slice on top of each cutlet, moulding the persillade slightly to help it stay in place. Squeeze excess water from the caul, then cut into six pieces and wrap each cutlet in caul. Return the wrapped cutlets to the baking tray and bake for 8–10 minutes. Remove, cover loosely with foil and leave to rest on the tray for 10 minutes.

Meanwhile, heat the butter and a little olive oil in a frying pan over medium heat and pan-fry the mushrooms for 4–5 minutes, then season to taste. Gently reheat the mashed potato, if required.

To serve, place a cutlet on each plate, with the mushrooms to one side. Pour the Madeira sauce over the top and garnish with sprigs of chervil or parsley.

Serves 6

wine
I would recommend a ripe, juicy, fruit-driven red wine, such as a Spanish tempranillo. These wines are medium-bodied and have distinctive notes of aniseed and spice.

Veal Saltimbocca with Risotto Milanese

18 × 50 g slices veal loin or escalopes
18 sage leaves
9 slices prosciutto, cut in half lengthways
pepper
a little olive oil

Risotto Milanese
3 litres chicken stock
2 pinches saffron threads

125 g shelled peas, from 250 g peas in pods
100 ml olive oil
10 golden shallots, finely diced
1 clove garlic, finely chopped
500 g risotto rice
salt and pepper
125 g mascarpone
50 g parmesan, finely grated

Literally translated, saltimbocca means 'jump in your mouth', and the flavours of sage and prosciutto really do make your mouth jump in anticipation for the next tasty bite. Served with risotto, this is traditionally a winter dish, but I also love to serve it at other times of the year, replacing the risotto with a salad of radicchio, fennel and lemon. Buy the palest-coloured veal you can find.

For the risotto Milanese, place the chicken stock and saffron in a saucepan, then bring to the boil and boil for approximately 30 minutes or until reduced by half; keep hot. Blanch the peas in a saucepan of boiling water for 1 minute, then drain and refresh under cold running water. Heat the olive oil in a large saucepan and sauté the shallots and garlic for approximately 1–2 minutes or until translucent, without browning. Add the rice and cook, stirring constantly, for approximately 1–2 minutes; once again, do not allow to brown. Add the hot chicken stock to the rice mixture, one third at a time, each time stirring until the rice has absorbed the liquid. Each third should take approximately 6 minutes to be absorbed, so the total cooking time should be around 18 minutes. Season to taste with salt and pepper. Stir the mascarpone, parmesan and peas through the risotto just before serving.

Place each slice of veal between two sheets of plastic film, then flatten slightly, using a rolling pin. Put one sage leaf on each piece followed by a piece of prosciutto, pressing down lightly. Repeat with remaining veal slices, sage and prosciutto, then season with pepper. Heat a little oil in a large frying pan until hot, then add the veal, prosciutto-side down, and pan-fry for 1 minute. Turn and pan-fry the other side for another minute.

Spoon the hot risotto onto six plates and top with the veal saltimbocca.

Serves 6

wine
Veal dishes are generally suited to red wines that are medium in palate weight and not too tannic. I would serve a savoury cabernet sauvignon with blackcurrant, cedar, vanilla and mint flavours.

Roast Lamb Leg with Preserved Lemon and Chargrilled Vegetables

2 kg lamb leg (ask your butcher to de-bone and truss it for you)
1 clove garlic, cut into slivers
80 g preserved lemon (see page 210), flesh discarded and rind chopped
6 rosemary sprigs
30 ml olive oil
salt and pepper
3 potatoes, unpeeled
3 cloves garlic, unpeeled

finely grated zest of 1 lemon
3 red peppers
300 g chat potatoes, scrubbed and cut in half
1 bunch baby carrots, trimmed and scrubbed
50 ml olive oil
3 red onions, cut into quarters
1 bunch baby leeks, trimmed
1 bunch asparagus
a little strained lemon juice, to serve

With this dish, it is important that you get the garlic, lemon and rosemary right into the incisions in the lamb, to infuse the meat with the delicious flavours and aromas. The lamb is roasted on a bed of potatoes for two reasons: firstly, they prevent the lamb from drying out and sticking to the pan; and secondly, they become crisp and incredibly tasty as they absorb all the cooking juices from the lamb.

Preheat the oven to 180°C. Using a sharp knife, make small incisions all over the leg and insert slivers of garlic, preserved lemon and the leaves from half the rosemary. Rub with olive oil and season liberally.

Roughly cut the unpeeled potatoes into small cubes and place in a large roasting tin. Using the flat of a knife, lightly crush the unpeeled garlic cloves and add to the potatoes, along with the lemon zest and the remaining rosemary. Place the lamb on top of the potatoes and roast for approximately 1½ hours for medium-rare (if you have a meat thermometer, it should read 55–60°C).

While the lamb is cooking, prepare the vegetables. Blacken the peppers over a naked flame or under a hot grill, then place in a bowl, cover with plastic film and leave for 10 minutes. Peel off the blackened skin and discard. Cut each pepper in half, remove the seeds and cut the flesh into strips.

Bring a large saucepan of salted water to the boil. Add the halved chat potatoes and simmer for 5–8 minutes, then remove and transfer to a bowl. Add the baby carrots to the simmering water and cook for 3 minutes. Drain and add to the bowl with the potatoes, then toss with a little olive oil and salt and pepper. In another bowl, toss the onions, leeks and asparagus with a little olive oil and salt and pepper. Heat the barbecue.

When the lamb is ready, remove from the oven, cover loosely with foil, and leave to rest for 20 minutes.

Meanwhile, chargrill all the vegetables on a hot chargrill pan or the grill plate of your barbecue, turning them a couple of times, until cooked.

To serve, place the lamb on a platter, surround with the vegetables and squeeze over a little lemon juice. Use a very sharp knife to carve the lamb into slices about 1.5 cm thick.

Serves 6

wine
I can't go past a good-value bottle of Chianti Classico Riserva. These wines are savoury and sweet at the same time, with flavours such as cherries, plums, leather and mushrooms. My favourite producers include Carpineto, Fattoria Felsina and Casa Sola.

Poached Lamb Loin with Basil Mousse and Lentils

6 × 180 g lamb loin fillets or backstraps, trimmed of sinew
salt and pepper
1 tablespoon olive oil
12 large silverbeet leaves, blanched and ribs removed

Lentils
50 g duck fat or lard
100 g bacon, diced
1 carrot, finely diced
1 celery stalk, finely diced
1 onion, finely diced
12 cloves garlic, peeled
2 thyme sprigs
1 bay leaf

200 g Puy-style lentils
400 ml chicken stock
3 baby carrots, scrubbed and sliced
40 g shelled peas, from 80 g peas in pods
2 tablespoons black olives, pitted and chopped
salt and pepper

Chicken and basil mousse
2 bunches basil, leaves picked
1 bunch spinach, leaves picked
125 g chicken breast fillet, well-chilled
2 egg whites, chilled
150 ml cream, chilled
salt and pepper

This dish is a little more challenging than some of my other recipes, but definitely no less rewarding – its success is dependent on careful construction of the lamb parcels, and allowing the lamb time to rest. The Puy-style lentils have a wonderful nutty flavour and don't take too long to cook; the basil mousse could also be slipped under the skin of a poached chicken breast prepared in the same way.

To make the lentils, preheat the oven to 180°C. In a large ovenproof saucepan or flameproof casserole, melt the duck fat or lard and cook the bacon, carrot, celery, onion, garlic, thyme and bay leaf for 2–3 minutes or until the vegetables have softened; do not allow to brown. Rinse the lentils in cold water, then add to the pan, along with the stock, and bring to the boil. Cover the saucepan with foil and braise in the oven for 10–15 minutes. Meanwhile, bring a saucepan of water to the boil, and blanch the baby carrots for 2–3 minutes and the peas for 1 minute, then drain and refresh under cold running water. Check the lentils; they should be soft but not mushy. Stir through the carrots, peas and olives, then season with salt and pepper to taste.

To make the chicken and basil mousse, blanch the basil and spinach leaves in a large saucepan of boiling salted water for 30 seconds, then refresh under cold running water. Purée in a food processor, then transfer to a bowl. Place the chicken in the food processor and process to a fine mince. Add the egg whites, process again, then slowly add the cream, pulsing after each addition, until a nice glossy texture is achieved (don't over-blend as the heat generated will cook the chicken). Transfer to the bowl containing the basil and spinach and stir to combine, then season with salt and pepper, cover and refrigerate until required.

Remove the loin meat from the bone, trim away any sinew, and season the meat with salt and pepper. Heat the oil in a frying pan until hot, then add the loins and sear over high heat for 1–2 minutes on each side. Remove and allow to cool. Divide the mousse between the lamb loins and wrap each one in silverbeet leaves. Firmly wrap the lamb parcels in plastic film, tying a knot at each end. Steam the lamb loins in a steamer placed over boiling water for 8–10 minutes, then remove and rest for 10 minutes.

To serve, snip the knots at each end of the lamb parcels, remove the plastic film and cut each lamb loin into three slices. Divide the lentils among six plates and top each with three slices of lamb loin.

Serves 6

wine
I think a rich, dark pinot noir from Victoria would really suit this dish – especially one with spicy plum flavours, such as those produced by Bass Philip in Gippsland, or Mount Mary and De Bortoli in the Yarra Valley.

Lamb Shanks with Baby Vegetables and Rosemary Roast Potatoes

6 large lamb shanks, French-trimmed
50 ml olive oil
1 onion, diced
2 celery stalks, diced
2 carrots, diced
3 cloves garlic, sliced
5 thyme sprigs
1 teaspoon coriander seeds, roasted
1 teaspoon cumin seeds, roasted
pinch saffron threads, soaked in hot water for 5 minutes
300 g mango chutney, preferably Sharwood's Green Label
1 bay leaf
5 egg tomatoes, peeled, quartered and deseeded
400 ml red wine
2 litres chicken stock

Rosemary roast potatoes
750 g desiree potatoes, peeled and cut into 2 cm chunks
100 ml olive oil
4 cloves garlic, crushed
2 rosemary sprigs, leaves picked
salt and pepper

Baby vegetables
18 pearl onions, trimmed and peeled
18 baby turnips, trimmed and peeled
18 baby carrots, trimmed and peeled
18 asparagus spears, trimmed
18 baby green beans, trimmed
20 g butter, melted
salt and pepper

Lamb shanks are the ultimate comfort food and this recipe is an updated version of the classic 'meat and two veg'. The baby vegetables retain their natural sugars and are deliciously sweet. If you have any sauce left over from this dish, allow it to cool slightly, then pour into ice-cube containers and freeze. If you ever need a little lamb sauce in a hurry, just pop a couple of cubes out into a pan, along with a splash of wine and some herbs, and you have a ready-made sauce close at hand.

Season the lamb shanks with salt and pepper. Heat a little oil in a large heavy-based saucepan, then add the lamb shanks and brown all over. Remove from the pan and set aside. Add the onion, celery and carrots to the same pan and cook, stirring occasionally, for 4–5 minutes or until golden. Add the garlic, thyme, coriander and cumin seeds, saffron, chutney, bay leaf and tomatoes and cook for another 2 minutes, then add the wine and stock. Return the shanks to the saucepan, bring to the boil, then reduce the heat and simmer for 3 hours or until the lamb is tender (the meat should be just falling off the bone). Carefully transfer the lamb shanks to a bowl and keep warm. Strain the liquid through a fine sieve placed over a clean saucepan, then simmer for 15–20 minutes until reduced to a sauce consistency, skimming any fat from the surface.

While the lamb sauce is reducing, prepare the vegetables. For the rosemary roast potatoes, preheat the oven to 200°C.

Place the potatoes in a saucepan of cold, salted water, then bring to the boil and cook for approximately 5 minutes or until just tender. Drain the potatoes and leave in the saucepan, uncovered, to steam-dry for 5 minutes. Heat the olive oil in a roasting tin over high heat, and add the potatoes, garlic and rosemary. Season with salt and pepper, then transfer to the oven and roast for 5–10 minutes or until golden brown.

For the baby vegetables, bring a large saucepan of water to the boil. Cook the pearl onions for 5 minutes, the turnips for 3 minutes, the carrots for 2–3 minutes, and the asparagus and green beans for 1–2 minutes, then drain, toss with the butter and season.

To serve, place a lamb shank on each plate, spooning over some of the sauce. Surround with the baby vegetables, and serve the rosemary roast potatoes on the side.

Serves 6

wine
This is a rich, robust dish which cries out for a bold red wine. Go for a gutsy Aussie shiraz from the Barossa Valley. Yalumba, Peter Lehmann and Rockford all make terrific dense, chocolatey, full-blooded ones.

Roast Pork Loin with Baked Apples

1.2 kg pork loin, preferably Kurobuta, rind removed
    and loin trussed (ask your butcher to do this)
salt and pepper
celery leaves, to serve

Pommes dauphine – optional
250 g chat potatoes
100 g unsalted butter
½ teaspoon salt
150 g plain flour, sieved
4 eggs
salt and pepper
pinch nutmeg
vegetable oil, for deep-frying

Sauce Robert (mustard sauce)
200 g chicken wings, chopped (ask your butcher to do this)
50 ml olive oil
1 clove garlic, thinly sliced
4 golden shallots, thinly sliced
1 thyme sprig
1 bay leaf
50 ml chardonnay vinegar
250 ml chicken stock
250 ml veal jus (see page 211)
1 tablespoon Dijon mustard

This is a sexy version of roast pork and apple sauce. I prefer
to use Kurobuta pork, which is produced from an old English
breed of pig, raised near Byron Bay in northern New South Wales.
It has fat marbling throughout, so the meat retains moisture and
flavour after cooking. While I serve this with pommes dauphine
at ARIA, at home I might serve it more simply with roast or
mashed potatoes.

If making the pommes dauphine, place the potatoes in
a saucepan of cold water, then bring to the boil and simmer
for 10 minutes or until tender. Drain the potatoes and leave
them in the saucepan, uncovered, to steam-dry for 10 minutes.
Using your fingers, peel the potatoes and push them through
a fine sieve placed over a bowl to purée.

Make a choux pastry by bringing 250 ml of water, the
butter and salt to the boil in a heavy-based saucepan; cook for
1 minute, then remove from the heat. Using a wooden spoon,
beat in the flour, then return the saucepan to medium heat and
cook for 3–4 minutes, stirring constantly, until the batter pulls
away from the sides of the pan and forms a ball. Remove from
the heat and allow to cool for 5 minutes. Transfer the batter
to a food processor and, with the motor running, add the eggs
one at a time, making sure each is fully incorporated before
adding the next, until you have a smooth, shiny batter. Stir

125 g of the choux pastry into the potato purée and season
with salt, pepper and nutmeg. The pommes dauphine can be
prepared in advance up to this point and refrigerated, covered
with plastic film, until needed.

Preheat the oven to 180°C. Season the pork loin with
salt and pepper then transfer it to a hot roasting tin, place
in the oven and roast for 45 minutes (if you have a meat
thermometer, it should register 55°C).

While the pork is cooking, make the sauce Robert. Place
the chopped chicken wings and the olive oil in a roasting tin
and roast in the oven for approximately 5 minutes or until
golden. Add the garlic, shallots, thyme and bay leaf to the
roasting tin, then place over medium heat and cook, stirring
occasionally, for 5–6 minutes or until brown. Add the vinegar
and then simmer for 5 minutes until the mixture is reduced
by half. Add the chicken stock and veal jus to the pan and
leave to simmer for about 15–20 minutes, or until the sauce
thickens to a sauce consistency. Stir in the mustard, then strain
the sauce through a fine sieve placed over a bowl; transfer to
a sauceboat or jug and keep warm.

Remove the pork from the oven and leave to rest for
20 minutes in a warm place. >

Apple purée
25 ml rice wine vinegar
10 g castor sugar
1 vanilla bean, split
3 green apples, peeled, cored and finely sliced
juice of ½ lemon, strained

Caramelised apples
4 green apples, peeled and cored
2 lemons, juiced
80 g butter
80 g sugar

Meanwhile, make the apple purée and the caramelised apples. To make the apple purée, place the rice wine vinegar, sugar and vanilla bean in a saucepan, bring to the boil and simmer for about 5 minutes. Add the apples and lemon juice, then cook for a further 5 minutes. Remove from the heat and take out the vanilla bean before blending to a smooth purée with a hand-held blender. For the caramelised apples, cut each apple into six wedges, then carve each piece into a barrel shape, if desired. Place in a bowl with half the lemon juice and enough water to cover. Place the butter and sugar in a saucepan and cook over medium heat, stirring, for 2–3 minutes or until the mixture caramelises and turns a golden colour. Add the apples and cook, tossing occasionally, for another 5 minutes. Pour the rest of the lemon juice over the apples, and stir gently to form a caramel sauce.

If serving with pommes dauphine, use two oiled spoons to shape the mixture into quenelles, and place on a lightly oiled baking tray. Deep-fry the pommes dauphine at 180°C for 2–3 minutes until crisp and golden brown.

When ready to serve, gently reheat the apple purée. Remove the string from the pork and cut into 1.5 cm slices. Spoon a little of the warm apple purée onto each plate, then top with slices of pork. Place the caramelised apples and pommes dauphine on the side and garnish with the celery leaves. Accompany with the sauce Robert.

Serves 6

wine
I suggest a rich honeyed pinot gris from Alsace near the French–German border. These spicy, aromatic wines are quite rich and intense in the mouth. Their fruit flavour tends to be that of stewed pears.

Barbecued Beef Rolled in Herbs with Onion Rings

500 g wagyu or other heavily marbled sirloin
salt and pepper
1 bunch flat-leaf parsley, finely chopped
1 bunch coriander, finely chopped
a little olive oil

1 red onion, thinly sliced into rings
60 g salted baby capers, rinsed and drained
handful baby coriander sprigs
handful baby shiso leaves
salsa verde (see page 210), and aïoli (see page 206), to serve

I love cooking on the barbecue, and this dish makes a great starter. Wagyu beef comes from a breed of cattle that originated in Japan. The meat these cows produce is renowned for its high fat content, which is marbled throughout the meat; this means that it retains moisture and flavour during the cooking process. It is important that the barbecue is very hot, so that the beef develops a blackened aromatic crust.

Preheat the barbecue to hot. Trim any excess fat from the sirloin then cut it in half lengthways and season with salt and pepper. Combine the parsley and coriander in a bowl then press the herb mixture all over the sirloin. Drizzle the meat with olive oil, then place on the hot barbecue and cook for 5 minutes on each side – the meat should be quite charred on the outside. Remove from the barbecue and allow to rest for 10 minutes before slicing as thinly as possible.

Lay the slices of sirloin on a platter and drizzle with olive oil. Scatter the onion rings, capers, baby coriander and baby shiso over the beef, then season to taste. Serve with salsa verde and aïoli on the side.

Serves 6

wine
I would serve a dry and savoury merlot with this dish. Some of the merlots from South Australia are suitably aromatic, with a silky-smooth texture and blackcurrant flavours dominating.

Sirloin Steak with Red Wine Butter and Pont Neuf Potatoes (Fat Chips)

50 ml olive oil
6 × 220 g aged sirloin steaks
120 ml veal jus (see page 211)
1 teaspoon finely chopped chives

Red wine butter
40 ml cabernet vinegar
40 ml merlot vinegar
750 ml red wine
1 large clove garlic, finely chopped
1 bay leaf
1 thyme sprig

5 black peppercorns
2 egg yolks
200 g unsalted butter, at room temperature
1 tablespoon flat-leaf parsley, finely chopped
1 tablespoon tarragon, finely chopped
1 tablespoon chives, finely chopped
salt and pepper

Pont neuf potatoes (fat chips)
1.5 kg large desiree potatoes
vegetable oil, for deep-frying

This is my version of that bistro classic, Steak Frites. Try to use good-quality grain-fed sirloin. The pont neuf potatoes, or 'fat chips', are wonderfully old-fashioned: hand-cut, crisp and golden on the outside, and white and fluffy on the inside. The red wine butter can be made in advance – it will keep for about 6 months in the freezer – and any leftovers can be used to enrich stews and winter casseroles. If you can't find the red wine vinegars made from a single grape variety listed above, just use 80 ml red wine vinegar instead.

For the red wine butter, place the cabernet and merlot vinegars, red wine, garlic, bay leaf, thyme and peppercorns in a saucepan. Simmer over low heat for about 10–15 minutes, or until the mixture is reduced to a tenth of its original volume – around 50 ml. Allow to cool until it is just warm. In a heatproof glass or metal bowl placed over a saucepan of simmering water, whisk the egg yolks, then slowly add the reduced liquid, whisking continuously, until the mixture is frothy and thick enough to coat the back of a spoon; do not heat to more than 65°C or it will curdle. Cool the egg-yolk mixture to the same temperature as the soft butter, then gently fold in the butter using a whisk. Stir through the chopped herbs, season to taste and roll into a log, then wrap in plastic film and refrigerate for at least 1 hour until firm.

For the fat chips, peel and cut the potatoes evenly into rectangular shapes approximately 5 × 1.5 × 1.5 cm. Deep-fry the chips in batches in vegetable oil heated to 140°C in a deep-fryer or heavy-based saucepan for about 8 minutes, or until soft and tender, then remove from the oil. Reheat the oil to 190°C, then return the chips to the oil in batches, and deep-fry for 10 minutes or until golden brown. Drain on kitchen paper and keep warm.

Rub the steaks with olive oil and sear on a hot chargrill or barbecue for approximately 4–5 minutes on each side for medium-rare; cook for longer, if desired. Allow the steaks to rest for 5–8 minutes before serving. Meanwhile, heat the veal jus in a small saucepan until warmed through.

To serve, place a steak on each plate. Cut six slices from the log of red wine butter and place one on top of each steak, then spoon over a little jus and sprinkle with chives. Serve the chips alongside.

Serves 6

wine
I would suggest a cabernet shiraz blend from South Australia. These wines are typically robust with firm, drying tannins, and dominant flavours of blackcurrant, cloves, mint and chocolate.

Poached Beef Fillet with Foie Gras and Spinach

2 bunches spinach
6 × 180 g beef fillets, centre-cut from the eye fillet
salt and pepper
olive oil
120 g foie gras
1.5 kg mashed potato (see page 208)

Bordelaise sauce
30 ml olive oil
100 g chicken wings, chopped (ask your butcher to do this)
3 golden shallots, sliced
½ clove garlic, chopped
1 slice bacon, chopped
1 bay leaf
250 ml red wine
300 ml veal jus (see page 211)

Poaching beef intensifies its flavour and also keeps the meat more moist than roasting or pan-frying. This is a very traditional French dish, complete with the addition of foie gras in the centre of the fillet. It is a perfect main course for winter, and is sublime served sitting on a pillow of creamy mashed potato, finished with bordelaise sauce.

For the bordelaise sauce, heat the olive oil in a large saucepan until hot, then add the chicken wings and cook for 5 minutes or until golden brown. Add the shallots, garlic, bacon and bay leaf and cook over low heat, stirring, for 2–3 minutes or until they start to caramelise. Deglaze the pan with the red wine, then simmer for another 3–4 minutes or until reduced by half. Add the veal jus and bring it to the boil, reduce heat and simmer for 45 minutes, skimming away any scum from the surface. Strain the sauce through a fine sieve placed over a saucepan.

Blanch the spinach in a large saucepan of boiling salted water for 30 seconds, drain and refresh under cold running water, then lay out to dry on a clean tea towel. Season the beef with salt and pepper. Heat a little olive oil in a large frying pan until hot, then add the beef fillets and sear for about 1 minute on each side. Leave to cool. Cut the foie gras into

six 1 × 5 cm batons, then wrap each piece in a little spinach. Using the handle of a wooden spoon, make a deep pocket in the centre of each beef fillet, then push a spinach-wrapped foie gras baton into each pocket. Wrap each beef fillet in spinach to form a parcel and firmly wrap each parcel in plastic film, tying a knot in both ends. Poach the fillets in a large saucepan of boiling water for 8 minutes, then remove and allow to rest for 10 minutes.

Meanwhile, gently warm the bordelaise sauce and reheat the mashed potato.

To serve, place some mashed potato in the centre of each plate. Slice each beef parcel in half, then remove the plastic film and place both halves on top of the mash. Pour some bordelaise sauce around the plate.

Serves 6

wine

A stylish claret or Bordeaux-style blend would be appropriate here. A cabernet blended with malbec, merlot and petit verdot produces a savoury wine with subtle hints of blackcurrant, supported by notes of dried herbs, violets and tobacco.

Daube of Beef with Pancetta, Peas and Mash

1 litre red wine
1 large carrot, peeled and diced
1 leek, white part only, well-washed and diced
1 onion, diced
1 celery stalk, diced
5 thyme sprigs
1 bay leaf
4 cloves garlic, unpeeled but lightly crushed
    with the flat of a knife
6 beef cheeks

salt and pepper
a little olive oil
1 litre veal jus (see page 211)
500 ml chicken stock
2 tablespoons HP sauce
12 slices flat pancetta
125 g double-peeled broad beans, from 500 g beans in pods
125 g shelled peas, from 250 g peas in pods
1.5 kg mashed potato (see page 208)

Daube is just a fancy name for braised beef. I like to use beef cheeks in my version; they have a delicious, gelatinous texture and a rich, concentrated flavour after they have been slowly braised for hours. Any leftover meat is also great the next day, sliced and made into sandwiches with pickles. You'll need to pre-order the beef cheeks from your butcher.

Combine the wine, carrot, leek, onion, celery, thyme, bay leaf and garlic in a large bowl, then add the beef cheeks, cover with plastic film and leave to marinate for 6–8 hours in the refrigerator.

Preheat the oven to 160°C. Drain the cheeks from the marinade, reserving the liquid and season with salt and pepper. Strain the liquid over a bowl, reserving both vegetables and liquid. Heat a little oil in a large ovenproof pan or flameproof casserole dish until hot, then add the seasoned beef cheeks and sear on both sides. Add the strained vegetables and cook over medium heat for 5 minutes or until caramelised. Pour over the reserved marinade, bring to the boil, then simmer for 10–15 minutes or until the liquid is reduced by half. Add the veal jus, chicken stock and HP sauce, bring back to the boil, then simmer for 5 minutes, skimming any fat from the surface. Cover the pan with foil or a lid, transfer to the oven and cook for 3½ hours or until tender. Remove the daube from the oven, then increase the temperature to 180°C.

Carefully remove the beef cheeks from the pan (they will be very soft). Strain the cooking liquid through a fine sieve placed over a clean saucepan, then simmer for 10–15 minutes or until reduced to a sauce consistency.

Meanwhile, place the pancetta on a baking tray and bake for 8–10 minutes or until crispy. Cook the broad beans and peas in boiling water for 2–3 minutes, then drain. Gently reheat the mashed potato. Return the beef cheeks to the sauce and warm through.

To serve, spoon some mashed potato onto each plate, with some broad beans and peas alongside. Place a beef cheek on top and spoon some of the sauce around the plate, then place the pancetta on the beef cheek.

Serves 6

wine

A hearty winter dish such as this deserves a wine that is rich in savoury flavours like mushrooms and bacon rind. I would recommend an aged Hunter Valley shiraz. These wines characteristically age beautifully to display notes of spice, leather and game.

Cassoulet

Duck confit
6 thyme sprigs
150 g table salt
15 g five-spice powder
8 duck legs
1 kg duck fat

700 g dried white haricot beans,
    soaked overnight in cold water
50 ml olive oil
150 g butter
2 large carrots, finely diced
2 celery stalks, finely diced
4 onions, finely diced
3 cloves garlic, finely diced
3 thyme sprigs
500 ml dry red wine
400 g pork belly
4 chorizo sausages
2 cotechino sausages

This dish is a labour of love, but the time spent on preparation is well worth it. Like most braises or stews, cassoulet tastes even better the next day, once all the flavours have integrated. The dish should be cooked in a large ovenproof earthenware or enamelled cast-iron casserole with a lid, such as a Le Creuset. If you are reheating this dish, do it slowly and make sure the crust is golden and crisp. A simple green salad, and perhaps a warm baguette, is all you need as accompaniments. If you don't have time or inclination to make duck confit, you can buy it from speciality food stores – you'll need eight confit duck legs for this dish. Cotechino sausages are available from Italian butchers and some delicatessens; duck fat can be purchased from speciality food shops.

If making your own duck confit, chop the thyme and mix with the salt and spice. Rub the duck legs with the salt mix, place in a bowl and leave to marinate for 2–3 hours in the refrigerator. Preheat the oven to 100°C. Under cold running water, rinse the salt mixture off the duck legs, then pat them dry with kitchen paper. Place the duck legs in a roasting tin, cover with the duck fat and bake for 8 hours. Remove the duck legs from the fat and, when cool enough to handle, separate the meat from the bones, shredding it with your fingers, and set aside in the fridge until ready to use. (The duck fat can be re-used for your next batch of confit – just sieve to remove impurities and store in the fridge.)

If using bought duck confit, simply remove the meat from the bones and shred with your fingers.

Drain and rinse the soaked haricot beans, then place in a large saucepan and cover with cold water. Bring to the boil, then turn down the heat and simmer for 30 minutes or until soft. Drain and set aside.

Meanwhile, heat half of both the olive oil and butter in an earthenware or enamelled cast-iron casserole dish over medium heat and cook the carrots, celery, onions, garlic and thyme for 6–8 minutes or until the vegetables are soft. Add the red wine, increase the heat to high, and cook for 15–20 minutes or until the liquid is reduced by a third. Transfer the contents of the casserole dish to a large bowl and set aside.

Cut the pork belly and all the sausages into 2 cm slices. Return the casserole dish to medium–high heat and fry the pork belly and sausages in their own fat for 5 minutes or until well browned. >

1 litre veal jus (see page 211)
1 bouquet garni – 2 bay leaves, 3 sprigs thyme, 5 flat-leaf
    parsley sprigs and 1 celery stalk, cut into 7 cm lengths,
    all tied together with kitchen string
2 tablespoons orange marmalade
salt and pepper
1 large day-old baguette
2 cloves garlic, halved
2 heaped tablespoons chopped flat-leaf parsley
1 heaped tablespoon chopped thyme leaves

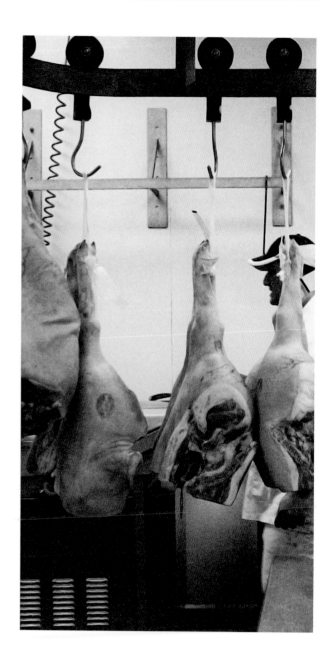

Add the veal jus and the drained beans to the casserole,
along with the reserved red wine reduction and sautéed
vegetables. Bring to the boil, then reduce the heat to low, add
the bouquet garni, marmalade and confit duck meat. Season
with a good amount of salt and pepper. Cover and leave to
simmer slowly for 2 hours, stirring occasionally.

About half an hour before the end of the cooking time,
preheat the oven to 180°C. Cut the crusts off the baguette,
tear the bread into pieces and use a blender or food processor
to make into coarse breadcrumbs. Heat the remaining olive
oil and butter in a frying pan over high heat, then add the
chopped garlic and breadcrumbs and cook until golden brown.
Remove from the heat, toss in the parsley and thyme, stir,
and season with salt and pepper. Remove the cassoulet from
the heat, scatter over the herb and breadcrumb mixture, then
transfer to the oven and bake for 15 minutes or until the crust
is crispy and golden.

Serves 8

wine

*I love to serve a rustic, savoury red wine with this dish. I would
recommend a wine from the Côtes du Rhone or Châteauneuf
du Pape regions of France. These wines are medium-bodied
but with firm tannins, plummy fruit and pepper and spice.
In Australia, the Barossa Valley produces some very good
grenache, shiraz and mourvedre blends, notably from Torbruck
and under the 'Nine Popes' label from Charles Melton, which
would also complement this earthy casserole.*

DESSERTS

Mandarin Jelly

30 g leaf gelatine
100 g castor sugar
900 ml strained mandarin juice, from about 15–20 mandarins
1 punnet raspberries
6 mint leaves, very finely shredded
baby basil leaves, to serve

Candied grapefruit peel
2 grapefruit
150 g castor sugar

Chocolate sauce
75 ml cream
180 g chocolate, chopped

When mandarins are in season, I like to buy a box and juice all of them. What I don't drink for breakfast, I make into this wobbly citric jelly. If you can't find raspberries to serve with the jelly, strawberries or blueberries are also fantastic with mandarin. The dots of chocolate sauce create that classic jaffa combination of chocolate and orange – I always use Valrhona chocolate, but any good-quality chocolate would work well. This is one dessert that is a surefire hit with the kids, as well as the adults.

To make the mandarin jelly, place the gelatine in a bowl, cover with cold water and leave to soak for 4–5 minutes, or until soft. Bring 100 ml of water and the sugar to a simmer in a saucepan, then remove from the heat and add the softened gelatine. Stir through the mandarin juice then pour the jelly into six individual dariole moulds (I use 10 × 7 cm pyramid-shaped ones), each with a capacity of about 150 ml. Leave the jelly to set in the refrigerator for at least 6 hours.

For the candied grapefruit peel, wash the grapefruit thoroughly before removing the peel in thin strips with a vegetable peeler, discarding any white pith. Blanch the strips of peel in a large saucepan of salted boiling water three times, refreshing under cold running water each time. Heat 150 ml of water and the sugar in a small saucepan until simmering, then add the grapefruit peel and simmer for 5 minutes. Remove from the heat and leave to cool, then strain.

For the chocolate sauce, place the cream in a small saucepan and bring to a simmer, then add the chocolate. Heat, stirring, until the chocolate is fully melted, then remove from the heat and slowly stir in 75 ml of warm water. Set aside at room temperature until needed.

To serve, dip each mandarin jelly mould in a bowl of hot water for 30 seconds then run a knife around the edge. Hold a plate upside down on the mould with the jelly in the centre, then turn over and carefully remove the mould. Halve the raspberries and place around the jelly, along with the mint, basil and candied grapefruit peel, then dot the chocolate sauce around the plate.

Serves 6

wine
To complement the citrus elements in this dish, I would suggest a slightly drier style from the Veneto region in Italy. Prosecco is a light semi-sparkling wine with a touch of pear and melon on the palate and a crisp, clean finish.

Mango Carpaccio with Lime Ice Cream

½ fresh coconut
8 mangoes
8 mint leaves, very finely shredded, to serve

Lime ice cream
625 ml thickened cream
finely grated zest of 1 lime
7 egg yolks
60 ml lime juice, strained
30 ml limoncello – optional
185 g castor sugar

Candied lime peel
3 limes
100 g castor sugar

Passionfruit glaze
25 g castor sugar
6 passionfruit

This dessert is simple to prepare and makes an ideal finish to a lazy Sunday lunch. The three key flavours of mango, lime and passionfruit are a tropical palate-awakening. As George from *Seinfeld* exclaimed on tasting his first mango, 'This is like a taste explosion!'

Limoncello is an Italian lemon liqueur – it adds an extra burst of citrus flavour to the lime ice cream in this dessert, but is not essential.

For the lime ice cream, whisk the cream until it forms soft peaks, then cover and refrigerate. Place the lime zest in a bowl, along with the egg yolks, and whisk until thick and pale. In a small saucepan, bring the lime juice, limoncello (if using) and sugar to a simmer. Once the sugar has completely dissolved, remove the syrup from the heat and slowly pour into the yolk and zest mixture, whisking continuously. Allow to cool, then fold in the cream. Pour into a metal container and freeze, or churn in an ice-cream machine according to the manufacturer's instructions. Remove the ice cream from the freezer 5 minutes before serving to soften, if required.

For the candied lime peel, wash the limes thoroughly before removing the peel in large strips, using a vegetable peeler; discard any white pith. Blanch the peel in a saucepan of salted boiling water three times, refreshing under cold running water each time, then cut into thin strips. In a small saucepan, bring 100 ml of water and sugar to the boil, then add the lime peel and simmer for 5 minutes. Allow to cool before refrigerating until needed.

Meanwhile, for the passionfruit glaze, dissolve the castor sugar in 25 ml of hot water, then leave to cool. Cut each passionfruit in half and scrape out the pulp, then whisk the pulp into the syrup.

Preheat the oven to 120°C. Using a vegetable peeler, shave the fresh coconut flesh into 3 cm pieces, then place on a baking tray and toast in the oven for about 5 minutes, or until lightly browned at the edges.

To serve, slice the peeled mangoes as thinly as possible and fan around the plate. Drizzle with a little passionfruit glaze, then place a scoop of the lime ice cream in the centre and scatter with the candied lime peel, mint and toasted coconut.

Serves 8

wine
Because this dish has a high level of acidity from the passionfruit glaze and the lime in the ice cream, I would serve a late-picked Clare Valley riesling with some sweetness and honeyed qualities.

Vanilla Panna Cotta with Cherries

360 ml milk
85 g castor sugar
1 vanilla bean, split and seeds scraped
12 g leaf gelatine
360 ml yoghurt
30 cherries, halved

Cherry soup
500 g cherries, stoned and coarsely chopped
80 g castor sugar
75 ml red dessert wine (see 'wine' below) *or* port

Cherries are a very sensual fruit, especially when they are poached and served as a fragrant soup. Coupled with a quivering vanilla panna cotta, this is my interpretation of a classic Italian dessert. Serve with biscotti or a thin, crisp tuille biscuit for a contrasting crunchy texture.

For the panna cotta, heat the milk with the sugar and vanilla bean in a saucepan over low heat until hot; do not allow to boil. Take off the heat and leave to infuse for 30 minutes before removing the vanilla bean. Reheat the milk until hot, again taking care that it does not boil, then remove from the heat. Place the gelatine in a bowl, cover with cold water and leave to soak for 4–5 minutes or until soft, then remove. Add the softened gelatine to the milk and stir until it has completely dissolved, then stir in the yoghurt. Pour into six moulds approximately 7.5 cm diameter and 5.5 cm high, each with a capacity of about 150 ml, and leave to set in the fridge overnight.

To make the cherry soup, place the chopped cherries and sugar in a saucepan, then simmer until the sugar has dissolved.

Add 400 ml of water and bring back to a simmer, then take off the heat and process to a rough purée with a hand-held blender. Leave to stand for 1 hour, then stir in the dessert wine, before straining through a muslin-lined sieve placed over a bowl; do not force any cherry pulp through.

Remove the panna cotta from the moulds by dipping each mould in a bowl of hot water for 3 seconds to loosen the panna cotta, then carefully turn out into a shallow bowl. Place some halved cherries around the plate and pour the soup around the panna cotta.

Serves 6

wine

I would serve an Italian semi-sweet red dessert wine, such as a recioto-style valpolicella. This style of wine can be used to poach the cherries, and an extra glass makes a perfect accompaniment, and is also ideal for dunking biscotti into . . .

Raspberry Tart

3 punnets raspberries

Pastry
600 g plain flour
360 g unsalted butter
180 g icing sugar
2 eggs

Sesame and poppy seed nougatine
100 g unsalted butter
100 g castor sugar
35 ml liquid glucose
35 ml milk
100 g sesame seeds
35 g poppy seeds

White chocolate cream
375 g Valrhona white chocolate
3 egg yolks
750 g thickened cream, whipped

I just love the flavour of white chocolate with fresh raspberries, and the sesame and poppy seed nougatine adds an extra savoury dimension. One important tip is to always make sure that you rest the pastry before baking, otherwise it will shrink and toughen on cooking.

For the pastry, mix together the flour, butter and icing sugar in a food processor until it resembles breadcrumbs. With the motor running, add the eggs and process until a smooth dough forms, then wrap in plastic film. Leave to rest for 4 hours in the refrigerator.

Meanwhile, make the sesame and poppy seed nougatine. Bring the butter, sugar, glucose and milk to the boil in a small saucepan. Remove from the heat, stir in the sesame and poppy seeds and leave to cool. Preheat the oven to 160°C. Line a baking tray with greaseproof paper, spread out the nougatine as thinly as possible, then bake for approximately 10 minutes or until golden. Remove from the oven and set aside to cool, but leave the oven on, ready to bake the tart shell.

To make the tart shell, lightly grease a 35 × 11 cm rectangular tart tin, preferably with a removable base. Roll out the pastry on a lightly floured surface, then ease it into the tin, gently pressing it into the corners and trimming the edges with a knife. Fill with pastry weights, dried chickpeas or rice, and blind-bake for 15 minutes. Remove the pastry weights and bake for another 5 minutes or until golden. Leave the tart shell to cool, then carefully remove from the tin.

For the white chocolate cream, place the chocolate in a heatproof bowl set over saucepan of hot water and stir until melted, then whisk in the egg yolks and 45 ml of hot water. Fold in the whipped cream, cover with plastic film, and refrigerate until needed.

To serve, spoon the white chocolate cream into the tart shell. Arrange the raspberries in rows on the white chocolate cream, then break the cooled nougatine into small pieces and sprinkle over the tart.

Serves 6–8

wine

As ripe raspberries are delicate and have a slightly acidic finish, I would recommend a lighter style of dessert wine, such as an Italian Moscato d'Asti. These wines exude aromatic flavours of white peach and nectarine, and have a light spritz, or what the Italians call frizzante, *which makes the wine almost dance across your tongue.*

Caramelised Figs with Goat's Curd and Fig Caramel Sauce

75 g egg whites, from 2–3 eggs
35 g castor sugar
225 g goat's curd
6 figs
100 g castor sugar
1 bunch dried muscatels

Fig caramel sauce
1½ figs
120 g castor sugar

Fig jam
4 figs
100 g castor sugar

Honey tuiles
40 g unsalted butter
50 g icing sugar
85 g honey
60 g plain flour

There is nothing like eating a ripe, juicy fig at the height of their season in summer. In this dessert, the sweetness of the caramelised figs contrasts beautifully with the acidic, lemony flavour of the fresh goat's curd. Any leftover fig jam is delicious spread on toasted fruit bread for breakfast.

For the fig caramel sauce, purée the figs in a blender and set aside. Combine the sugar and 30 ml of water in a small heavy-based saucepan over low heat. Use a wet pastry brush to wash any sugar from the sides of the saucepan. Once the sugar has completely dissolved, increase the heat to high and cook, without stirring, until the caramel is a light golden colour. Carefully stir in the fig purée and 60 ml of water, and cook the sauce until the caramel has dissolved. Strain the sauce through a muslin-lined sieve placed over a bowl, and leave to cool before using.

To make the fig jam, roughly chop the figs into 1 cm pieces, then place in a saucepan with the sugar and cook over medium heat, stirring occasionally, for 10–15 minutes or until most of the moisture has evaporated to give the mixture a jam-like consistency. Remove from the heat and leave to cool.

For the honey tuiles, cream the butter and sugar until thick and pale. Mix in the honey, then stir through the flour. Leave the mixture to rest for 1 hour at room temperature. Preheat the oven to 160°C. Line a baking tray with baking paper, then spread the mixture into six 6 cm × 1 mm rounds (any leftover tuile mixture will keep in the fridge for up to 2 weeks). Bake the tuiles for approximately 10 minutes or until they are a deep golden colour. Leave to cool.

Whisk the egg whites in a bowl until soft peaks form, then gradually add the 35 g of sugar, and whisk until stiff peaks form. Gently fold the goat's curd into the egg whites, cover with plastic film, and store in the fridge until needed.

Just before serving, cut the figs in half and sprinkle the cut side with the 100 g of sugar. Caramelise the sugar with a blow torch or under a very hot grill. Spoon some goat's curd onto each plate. Place two caramelised fig halves alongside and spoon a little fig jam next to them. Scatter a few of the dried muscatels around the plates, then drizzle with a little fig caramel sauce and place a honey tuile on top of the figs.

Serves 6

wine
I would recommend a lighter style of fortified wine, such as a tokay or tawny port, to drink with this dessert.

Ginger Crème Brûlée with Pineapple Confit

140 g egg yolks, from 8 eggs
110 g castor sugar
560 ml cream
60 ml fresh ginger juice
15 g leaf gelatine, softened in cold water
480 ml thickened cream
4 sheets filo pastry
100 g unsalted butter, melted
100 g icing sugar, plus extra for serving

Pineapple confit
1 golden rough pineapple, peeled and cut into 1 cm dice
150 g castor sugar
50 g unsalted butter
½ vanilla bean, split and seeds scraped

Caramel sauce
200 g castor sugar
200 ml pineapple juice

Frosted pistachios
50 g castor sugar
30 pistachios

Much of the preparation for this dessert can be done the day before. To extract ginger juice from fresh ginger, either peel and run through a juicer, or place finely grated ginger in muslin and squeeze by hand.

For the ginger brûlée, whisk the egg yolks and sugar in a bowl until thick and pale, then set aside. Put the cream and ginger juice in a small saucepan and bring to a simmer, then add the yolk mixture to the pan and slowly cook over low heat until the custard thickens enough to coat the back of a spoon. Add the softened gelatine and stir until completely dissolved, then strain the mixture through a muslin-lined sieve into a bowl and stir in the thickened cream. Pour the brulée mixture into a 30 × 23 × 4 cm baking tray lined with plastic film and leave in the fridge overnight to set, allowing a skin to form.

To make the pineapple confit, place all the ingredients in a saucepan and simmer, stirring occasionally, for 15–20 minutes or until most of the liquid has evaporated. Discard the vanilla bean and refrigerate the pineapple confit until needed.

For the caramel sauce, combine the sugar with 50 ml of water in a small, heavy-based saucepan over low heat. Use a wet pastry brush to wash any sugar from the sides of the saucepan. Once the sugar has completely dissolved, increase the heat and cook, without stirring, until the caramel is a light golden colour. Carefully add the pineapple juice and simmer, stirring continuously, until all the caramel has dissolved. Leave the sauce to cool to room temperature, then refrigerate.

The next day, make the bases for the crème brûlées. Preheat the oven to 170°C. Place a sheet of filo pastry on the bench top, brush with melted butter and sprinkle with icing sugar then lay another sheet of filo on top; repeat these layers with the remaining sheets of filo. Using a 7.5 cm diameter cutter, cut out six rounds of filo and place on a baking tray lined with baking paper. Place another sheet of baking paper on top, then weight down with another baking tray the same size, and bake for 8 minutes or until the pastry is golden.

Meanwhile, make the frosted pistachios: bring 50 ml of water and the castor sugar to the boil in a small saucepan, stir in the nuts and cook for 5–10 minutes until the sugar crystallises (but do not allow to colour). Remove and leave to cool.

To serve, use a 7.5 cm diameter cutter to cut six rounds of ginger crème and place one on top of each filo pastry round. Sprinkle with a little extra icing sugar and caramelise with a blowtorch. Pour a little caramel sauce onto each plate, then spoon on some pineapple confit. Place a ginger brûlée on top and scatter the pistachios alongside.

Serves 6

wine
I recommend a late-picked chenin blanc from the Loire Valley, in France. The appellation of Anjou produces wines that are very concentrated, with notes of cinnamon, spiced apples and vanilla.

Banana Tarte Tatin with Nutmeg Ice Cream

175 g castor sugar
50 g unsalted butter, diced
6 bananas
2 sheets frozen puff pastry

Nutmeg ice cream
500 ml milk
1 teaspoon ground nutmeg
125 g egg yolks, from 7–8 eggs
110 g castor sugar
125 ml cream

To my mind this is a quintessential winter dessert – the ethereal combination of flaky puff pastry, caramelised bananas and creamy nutmeg ice cream is sublime. In the kitchen at ARIA we use small cast-iron frying pans as tarte tatin moulds, but any round tart tins about 8–10 cm wide and 2 cm deep would do.

First, make the nutmeg ice cream. Bring the milk and nutmeg to a simmer in a small saucepan, then turn off the heat and leave to infuse for 30 minutes. Whisk the egg yolks and sugar in a bowl until thick and pale, then stir into the milk. Cook the custard over low heat, stirring constantly, until it is thick enough to coat the back of a spoon. Strain the custard into a bowl sitting in a larger bowl full of ice, so that it cools rapidly. Stir in the cream, then churn in an ice-cream machine according to the manufacturer's instructions.

Preheat the oven to 180°C. Make the caramel base for the tartes by combining the sugar and 50 ml of water in a small heavy-based saucepan over high heat. Cook the syrup until it is golden, then remove the pan from the heat and whisk in the butter. Divide the caramel among six tarte tatin pans. Cut the bananas into 5 mm slices and place them on top of the caramel, arranging the slices in a single, slightly overlapping layer. Cut out six puff pastry rounds to fit the tarte tatin pans and place one in each pan, tucking the edges in, then bake for 20 minutes or until golden.

Gently turn out each warm tarte tatin by turning the pan upside-down and tapping the bottom; it should slide out. Place a tarte in the centre of each plate, top with a scoop of nutmeg ice cream and serve immediately.

Serves 6

Wine
To offset the richness of the caramelised banana and puff pastry, I would look towards a leaner, sweeter wine from a cool-climate region, such as Tasmania. Iced rieslings from the Coal River Valley have succulent honeysuckle on the palate and a vibrant acidity.

Crispy Date Cigars with Lemon Cream

4 sheets brik pastry, cut into thirds
100 g unsalted butter, melted
12 dates, pitted
60 g icing sugar

Lemon cream
2 eggs
120 g castor sugar
80 ml lemon juice, strained
finely grated zest of 2 lemons
150 g unsalted butter, diced
200 g thickened cream, whipped

These cigars are a simplified version of a longstanding dessert from ARIA. You could serve them as a dessert with fresh berries, berry coulis and some vanilla ice cream, or cut them into small pieces and serve them as a petit four with coffee.

You'll need brik pastry for this recipe. Most Middle Eastern delicatessens should have it; do not be tempted to substitute filo pastry, as it is too brittle.

First, make the lemon cream. Lightly mix the eggs and sugar in a bowl until sugar has dissolved; set aside. Place the lemon juice and zest in a small saucepan and bring to a simmer, then remove from the heat and whisk in the egg mixture. Return the saucepan to low heat and cook until the mixture thickens. Take the saucepan off the heat and whisk in the butter piece by piece. Leave to cool, then cover with plastic film and refrigerate. When ready to serve, fold in the whipped cream.

Preheat the oven to 175°C. Make tubes out of the pastry by brushing each sheet with melted butter and wrapping it around a metal tube approximately 1 cm thick (you could use an ovenproof pan handle or any stainless-steel tube). Bake the pastry for 10 minutes or until golden, then remove from the tube while still hot and leave to cool. Place the dates between two sheets of baking paper and, using a rolling pin, roll them out as thinly as possible. Remove the dates from the paper, trim to fit the pastry tubes neatly, then wrap one around each tube.

Put the lemon cream into a piping bag and pipe the cream into the date 'cigars'. Serve immediately.

Serves 4

wine

A Pedro Ximenez sherry from Spain would be brilliant with this dessert – my favourite is rich with the heady flavours of molasses, figs and caramel, and is produced by Valdespino. Alternatively, serve a glass of Averna on ice, with a twist of orange. This Italian liqueur has some herbal flavours and a minty character that works well with both the dates and the lemon cream.

Rhubarb Crumble

200 g unsalted butter
100 g castor sugar
260 g plain flour
double cream, lightly whipped, to serve

Pastry base
180 g unsalted butter
90 g icing sugar
1 egg
300 g plain flour, sifted

Rhubarb compote
9 rhubarb stalks, trimmed and diced
300 g castor sugar

Poached rhubarb
275 ml sparkling white wine
200 g castor sugar
5 rhubarb stalks, trimmed and cut into 7 cm lengths

To many people, rhubarb is inextricably linked to childhood comfort food. In this dish, some of the rhubarb is made into a compote and the rest is cut into batons and gently cooked to retain its shape. A cross between a tart and a crumble, this elegant dessert is guaranteed to convert all reluctant rhubarb eaters!

To make the pastry base, cream the butter and icing sugar in an electric mixer for 5 minutes. Mix in the egg, then stir in the flour until combined. Wrap the dough in plastic film and leave to rest in the fridge for 2 hours.

Meanwhile, make the rhubarb compote. Place the rhubarb and castor sugar in a saucepan then slowly stew, stirring occasionally, for about 10 minutes or until most of the moisture has evaporated and the rhubarb is quite soft and mushy. Remove from the heat and set aside to cool.

For the poached rhubarb, preheat the oven to 100°C. Place the sparkling wine, castor sugar and 250 ml of water in a saucepan and bring to the boil. Place the rhubarb in a baking dish, then pour over the warm wine mixture and cover with foil. Bake for 10 minutes, then check to see if it is cooked; it should be softened but still firm enough to retain its shape. If it is not soft enough, cook for a little longer.

Increase the oven temperature to 170°C. On a lightly floured surface, roll out the pastry to 5 mm thick, then cut into six 7 cm squares. Transfer to a baking tray lined with baking paper and bake for 10–12 minutes or until golden brown.

Increase the oven temperature to 180°C. For the crumble, combine the butter and sugar in an electric mixer, then add the flour and continue mixing until a crumble-like texture is obtained. Spread the crumble on a baking tray and bake for 10 minutes or until golden.

When ready to serve, place pastry bases on a work bench and arrange the poached rhubarb stalks on top, keeping them square with the pastry base. Carefully spread some rhubarb compote on top of the stalks then sprinkle with the crumble. (For a more formal presentation, build the rhubarb crumble in layers in a square mould.) Transfer each rhubarb crumble to a plate, place a spoonful of rhubarb compote alongside and serve with a small dish of whipped cream.

Serves 6

wine
The wine to accompany this dessert should not be too rich, but have a perfumed floral aroma redolent of roses or even musk. A current-release Muscat De Riversaltes would be excellent.

Grand Marnier Soufflé

25 g cornflour
15 g plain flour
125 ml milk
3 egg yolks
finely grated zest and strained juice of 1 orange
50 g castor sugar
50 ml Grand Marnier
1 teaspoon orange-infused oil, such as Boyajian

butter, for greasing soufflé dishes
100 g castor sugar, plus extra for coating soufflé dishes
300 g egg whites, from 10 eggs
icing sugar, to serve

Blood orange sorbet
150 g castor sugar
500 ml blood orange juice, strained

This is the first soufflé I learnt to make as an apprentice chef over twenty years ago – it is foolproof, and still tastes as good today as it did then. The trick to making soufflés is to make sure that all your utensils are spotlessly clean and dry, and that you have all the ingredients close at hand. The other thing to watch is that you must be gentle when folding the soufflé base through the beaten egg whites: the more vigorous you are, the more you will release the air trapped in the whipped egg whites and the more deflated your soufflé will be. Of course, if blood oranges are not in season, you can use regular oranges – and feel free to serve whipped cream or a dark chocolate ice cream on the side.

To make the blood orange sorbet, dissolve the sugar in 250 ml of the blood orange juice in a saucepan over low heat. Remove from the heat and stir in the rest of the blood orange juice and churn in an ice-cream machine according to the manufacturer's instructions. Freeze the sorbet until firm.

For the soufflé base, combine the cornflour, plain flour, 25 ml of the milk and one of the egg yolks in a small bowl. In a small saucepan, bring the remaining milk, orange zest and juice to the boil, then remove from the heat. Whisk in the cornflour mixture, then return to the stove and cook over low heat, stirring constantly, until the custard thickens. In a separate bowl, stir together the sugar and the rest of the egg yolks, then add to the orange custard in the pan and cook for another 2 minutes, whisking constantly. Remove from the heat and stir in the Grand Marnier and orange oil, then strain through a fine sieve placed over a bowl. Cover the mixture with plastic film and leave to cool.

Preheat the oven to 170°C. Grease six copper soufflé pots or 250 ml capacity ramekins with butter and coat with castor sugar. Place the egg whites in a bowl and whisk until they form soft peaks, then gradually add the sugar and continue whisking until they are stiff. Place the soufflé base in a large bowl and gently fold in half of the egg whites, then fold in the other half. Spoon the mixture into the soufflé pots or ramekins to fill them right to the top, level with a spatula, and bake for 8–10 minutes until well risen.

Dust the soufflés with icing sugar and serve with a scoop of blood orange sorbet to the side.

Serves 6

wine

Muscat de Beaumes de Venise is a delicious, lightly fortified dessert wine from the southern area of the Rhone Valley in France; Bernadins and Jaboulet are two of the best producers. Characteristically showing hints of honey on the palate, these wines have floral aromas ranging from violets to rose petals, but they are not too sweet and so will not dominate the flavour or texture of the soufflé.

Champagne Savarin with Poached Summer Fruits

25 ml milk
1 teaspoon honey
12 g fresh yeast *or* 6 g dried yeast
3 eggs
150 g plain flour
pinch salt
50 g unsalted butter, diced
mint sprigs, to serve

Champagne ice cream
250 ml champagne
110 g egg yolks, from 6–7 eggs
110 g castor sugar
250 ml milk
100 ml cream

Poached summer fruits
750 ml champagne
320 g castor sugar
3 peaches, halved and stone removed
6 plums, halved and stone removed
6 apricots, halved and stone removed
18 lychees, peeled and stone removed

Champagne soaking syrup
600 ml champagne
250 g castor sugar
½ vanilla bean, split and seeds scraped

Special savarin moulds are available from most good kitchenware shops.

For the champagne ice cream, place the champagne in a saucepan and bring to the boil, then carefully ignite to burn off the alcohol. When the flame goes out, remove from the heat and allow to cool slightly. Place the egg yolks and sugar in a bowl, and whisk until thick and pale, then whisk in the milk. Add this mixture to the champagne, and cook slowly over a low heat, stirring constantly, until the custard is thick enough to coat the back of a spoon. Strain into a bowl sitting in a larger bowl full of ice, so that the custard cools rapidly. Stir in the cream, then churn in an ice-cream machine according to the manufacturer's instructions.

For the poached fruit, make a syrup by putting the champagne and sugar into a large saucepan, together with 350 ml of water. Bring to a simmer, stirring until the sugar has completely dissolved. Transfer about a quarter of the syrup to a small saucepan, add the peaches and simmer gently for 10 minutes, or until tender. Allow to cool, then peel and cut into wedges. Place the plums, apricots and lychees in the large pan of simmering syrup, cover, then remove from the heat and leave for 5 minutes or until tender. Allow to cool, then peel the plums and apricots and cut all the fruit into wedges.

To make the savarins, place the milk, honey and yeast in a bowl. Whisk to a smooth paste, then whisk in the eggs. Place the flour and salt in an electric mixer and, with the motor running at low speed, add the yeast mixture and mix until a wet dough forms. Sprinkle the butter over the top of the dough, but do not mix in. Cover with cling wrap and leave in a warm place to rise for 40 minutes or until nearly doubled in volume. Mix in the butter and transfer the dough to a piping bag. Butter and flour the savarin moulds and place them on a baking tray, then pipe in just enough dough to quarter-fill the rings and leave to prove again – about 20 minutes. Preheat the oven to 170°C. When the savarins have doubled in volume, bake for 17 minutes, or until golden.

Meanwhile, make the champagne soaking syrup. Place the champagne, sugar and vanilla bean in a saucepan, together with 500 ml of water, and bring to the boil, stirring until the sugar has completely dissolved then take off the heat. Remove the hot savarins from their moulds, slip them into the pan of hot syrup and allow to soak for 2–3 minutes.

To serve, place a savarin in each bowl, pour over a little syrup, and surround with poached fruit. Garnish with mint sprigs, then place a scoop of champagne ice cream in the centre of the savarin and serve immediately.

Serves 6

wine
A dessert soaked in champagne deserves only one wine. In this case, I would recommend a demi-sec style of champagne, which is on the sweeter side.

Baked Winter Fruit Tart

45 g dried apples
35 g dates, pitted
100 g dried pears
130 g dried apricots
150 g prunes
100 g dried figs
1 teaspoon ground allspice
1 teaspoon ground cinnamon
100 ml brandy
200 g castor sugar

2 egg yolks
30 ml cream
pinch salt
350 g apricot conserve

Pastry
750 g plain flour
450 g unsalted butter
100 g icing sugar
1 egg

I first started making this tart as a 15-year-old, second-year apprentice, when I used to bake at least a dozen per week and sell them to the local café to supplement my paltry income! This tart is ideal served warm with a jug of warm custard.

Place all the dried fruit and spices in a bowl and add the brandy. Add enough hot water to cover the fruit, then cover and leave to soak for 24 hours in the refrigerator.

For the pastry, mix together the flour, butter and icing sugar in a food processor until it resembles breadcrumbs. With the motor running, add the egg and process until a smooth dough forms, then wrap in plastic film. Leave to rest for 2 hours in the refrigerator. On a lightly floured surface, roll out half of the pastry to 5 mm thickness and use it to line a greased 27 cm diameter tart tin, then place in the refrigerator. Roll out the other half of the pastry to 5 mm thickness and cut into 1 cm wide strips using a zig-zag cutter.

Preheat the oven to 170°C. Strain the fruit, reserving the soaking liquid. Roughly chop the fruit and set aside. Place the liquid in a saucepan, add the sugar and heat, stirring occasionally, until the syrup is a light golden brown. Moisten the fruit with a little of the syrup to help it stick together – at this stage, feel free to add more syrup or brandy to suit your taste. Spoon the fruit mixture into the tart shell and lace the pastry strips on top in a criss-cross pattern. Lightly whisk the egg yolks, cream and salt together and brush over the top of the pie. Bake for 35 minutes, or until the pastry is golden brown.

While the tart is still hot, bring the apricot conserve and 150 ml of water to the boil in a small saucepan, stirring until the conserve has completely dissolved, then brush over top of the tart to glaze.

Serves 8–10

wine

This dish is full of sweet spices and concentrated dried-fruit flavours. Botrytis semillon from the Riverina district of New South Wales is rich in flavours of stewed oranges and peaches, making it the perfect choice with this tart.

Chocolate Delice

400 g castor sugar
60 hazelnuts, roasted
vanilla ice cream, to serve

Caramel truffle
40 g castor sugar
140 ml cream
250 g couverture milk chocolate

Chocolate pastry
40 g cocoa powder
160 g plain flour
80 g icing sugar
½ teaspoon salt
80 g unsalted butter, diced
1 egg

This is the signature dish on the dessert menu at ARIA, and its success is dependent on the quality of the chocolate that you use. I prefer Valrhona, however if you use another chocolate, make sure it has a minimum of 70 per cent cocoa. This dessert is not for the faint-hearted cook or dinner guest: it has many components and is challenging to make, but at the same time it is sublime to eat! With this dish, I wanted to create a chocolate dessert that was a complex amalgam of milk and dark chocolate and a contrast of soft and crisp textures. The crisp, chocolate pastry base counterbalances the softness of the caramel and the silkiness of the chocolate mousse. The caramelised hazelnuts add another crunchy dimension and a scoop of creamy vanilla ice cream completes my ultimate chocolate indulgence.

First, make the caramel truffle. Place six metal rings (10 cm diameter × 2 cm high) on a baking tray lined with greaseproof paper. Combine the sugar and 20 ml of water in a small heavy-based saucepan over low heat. Use a wet pastry brush to wash any sugar from the sides of the saucepan. Once the sugar has completely dissolved, increase the heat to high and cook, without stirring, until the caramel is a light golden colour. Carefully add the cream and simmer, stirring constantly, until the caramel has completely dissolved. Place the chocolate in a bowl, add the caramel mixture and mix until fully incorporated. Pour the caramel truffle into the metal rings and refrigerate until needed.

For the chocolate pastry, sift the cocoa, flour, icing sugar and salt into a food processor. Add the butter and process until the mixture resembles breadcrumbs. Add the egg and mix for approximately 1 minute, then turn out onto a lightly floured bench and knead until smooth. Wrap in plastic and refrigerate for 2 hours. Preheat the oven to 180°C and line a baking tray with greaseproof paper. Remove the metal rings from the caramel truffle, which should be set by now. Roll out the chocolate pastry to 2–3 mm thickness and, using one of the metal rings as a cutter, cut out six rounds of pastry, place on the lined baking tray and bake for 5 minutes. Allow the pastry rounds to cool, then place one in the base of each ring on a baking tray lined with baking paper. Place a caramel truffle round on top of the chocolate pastry, then refrigerate while you make the mousse and the icing. >

Summer Pudding

1 loaf brioche
2 punnets strawberries, hulled and halved
1 punnet blueberries
2 punnets raspberries
1 punnet each strawberries, raspberries and
  blueberries, extra, to serve

Syrup
150 g castor sugar
750 g strawberries
250 g raspberries

This dessert is a great way to use up any berries you may have in the fridge. In this recipe I have used brioche, which is a buttery, slightly sweet bread, but you could also use day-old bread in the same way, as long as you cut the crusts off. You could also serve this with a generous dollop of lightly whipped sweetened cream.

First, make the syrup. Place the sugar and 225 ml of water in a small saucepan over low heat and stir until the sugar has completely dissolved, then remove from the heat and allow to cool. Put the strawberries, raspberries and sugar syrup in a blender or food processor and purée, then strain through a muslin-lined sieve placed over a bowl. Set aside a quarter of the syrup, to be served with the puddings.

Cut the brioche into twelve 1 cm thick slices. Using a 7 cm diameter ring mould, cut out the centre of each slice. Place six ring moulds 7 cm in diameter and 4 cm high on a tray, then place a round of brioche in the bottom of each mould. Arrange a layer of halved strawberries on top of the brioche rounds, then fill the moulds with the remaining berries. Top each pudding with a brioche round, then divide all except the reserved syrup equally among the puddings. As the syrup will run to the bottom, carefully turn the puddings over after 10 minutes, so that the top gets soaked with the syrup as well. Cover the puddings with plastic film and place another tray on top to weigh it down. Place the trays in the fridge for a few hours, until ready to serve.

Cut the extra strawberries into quarters, place in a bowl with the rest of the extra berries and gently toss them together. Place a pudding in the centre of each bowl, then remove the ring moulds. Pour the reserved syrup around the base of the pudding, then top with the mixed berries.

Serves 6

wine
I would recommend a late-harvest Moscatel from Malaga in southern Spain. This wine displays opulent flavours of white peach, with a hint of orange marmalade and honeycomb.

Baked Passionfruit Tartlets

1 egg yolk
150 g castor sugar
3 eggs
150 ml cream
200 ml strained passionfruit pulp, from about 20–30 passionfruit
icing sugar, to serve

Sweet pastry
225 g unsalted butter
100 g icing sugar
375 g plain flour
1 egg
1 egg yolk, lightly beaten

These tartlets are delicious and simple to make, and even easier to eat. With a luscious passionfruit filling that's lightly caramelised just before serving, they are irresistible. Homemade tarts just don't get any better than this, and you can substitute lemon, orange or even lime juice for the passionfruit.

For the pastry, mix the butter, sugar and flour in a food processor until it resembles breadcrumbs. With the motor running, add the egg and combine until a dough forms. Wrap in plastic film and allow to rest for 2 hours in the fridge.

Preheat the oven to 160°C. On a lightly floured surface, roll out the pastry to 3 mm thickness and use to line six 8 cm diameter tart tins, then place in the refrigerator for 20 minutes. Fill with pastry weights, dried chickpeas or rice, and blind-bake for 15 minutes. Remove the pastry weights and bake for another 5 minutes or until golden. While still warm, fill any cracks with leftover pastry, then brush the insides of the tartlet shells with the lightly beaten egg yolk and return to the oven for 3 minutes or until lightly browned. Remove from the oven and allow to cool.

Reduce the oven temperature to 120°C. To make the filling, lightly mix together the eggs, egg yolk and castor sugar in a bowl until sugar has dissolved. Stir in the cream and passionfruit juice and then strain through a fine sieve into a jug. Pour the filling into the tartlet shells and bake for 10–15 minutes until just set – the filling should still wobble slightly in the centre. Leave to cool to room temperature.

Just before serving, dust the tarts with icing sugar and caramelise with a blowtorch or under a very hot grill.

Serves 6

wine

A glass of sweet and unctuous French Sauternes, or even a rich, dessert-style semillon from the Hunter Valley or Riverina regions of New South Wales, would be ideal here. These wines display flavours of honeyed citrus with notes of toffee and caramel.

Madeleines

100 g unsalted butter
35 g honey
100 g icing sugar
40 g almond meal

40 g plain flour
4 egg whites
olive oil spray or butter, for greasing
a little castor sugar – optional (see method)

These madeleines are perfect with morning or afternoon tea. They're best served piping hot, straight from the oven – so, if possible, make the batter a couple of hours beforehand. Then, while your guests sip on a tea or coffee, you can quickly drop dollops of the mixture into the moulds.

Melt the butter and honey in a small saucepan, remove from the heat and allow to cool to body temperature. Combine the icing sugar, almond meal and flour in an electric mixer. With the motor running at low speed, slowly add the egg whites. Once all the egg whites are incorporated, gradually add the butter and honey mixture and combine well. Cover with plastic film and refrigerate for at least 1 hour.

Preheat the oven to 180°C. Lightly spray a madeleine tray with olive oil spray or grease with butter and sprinkle with castor sugar for a nice crunch. Half-fill the moulds with the batter and bake for 8 minutes, or until golden and well risen. Immediately turn out the madeleines onto a cooling rack. Serve while still warm.

Basic Recipes

Aïoli

This garlic-infused mayonnaise is perfect with raw vegetables, as well as with grilled fish and chicken. Any leftovers will keep in the fridge for up to 7 days.

Makes 200 g

200 g mayonnaise (see page 209)
1 clove garlic, crushed
2 tablespoons lemon juice, strained
salt and pepper

Mix all the ingredients together in a bowl and leave to infuse for 1 hour, then pass the aïoli through a fine sieve and season to taste.

Chicken jus

This concentrated chicken stock adds richness and depth of flavour to sauces. It will keep for 7 days in the fridge or up to 3 months in the freezer.

Makes about 1 litre

50 ml vegetable oil
1 kg chicken wings, roughly chopped
    (ask your butcher to do this for you)
1 carrot, diced
1 onion, diced
¼ celery stalk, chopped
200 ml white wine
1.5 litres chicken stock (see page 207)
2 cloves garlic, peeled and chopped
2 thyme sprigs

Heat the vegetable oil in a large saucepan or stockpot, add the chopped chicken wings and cook over high heat until golden brown, stirring occasionally. Pour off any excess fat then add the carrot, onion and celery, and cook for 2–3 minutes. Add the white wine and simmer until the liquid is reduced by half. Add all the other ingredients and simmer for 45–50 minutes, skimming occasionally. Strain through a fine sieve into a saucepan, then return to the heat and simmer over medium heat until the required consistency is reached.

Shellfish oil

You'll need to start making this shellfish-infused oil at least 3 days before you want to use it. Once made, it will keep in a sealed glass bottle in the fridge for 4–6 weeks and can be used to enhance seafood soups, salads and pasta dishes.

Makes 250 ml

250 ml olive oil
250 g prawn heads and shells
½ onion, chopped
½ carrot, chopped
½ celery stalk, chopped
½ leek, white part only, well-washed and chopped
½ fennel bulb, trimmed and chopped
1 red chilli, chopped
1 tablespoon tomato paste
1 tomato, chopped
20 ml brandy
1 star anise
1 bay leaf
1 thyme sprig
2 flat-leaf parsley sprigs
salt and pepper

Place 100 ml olive oil in a saucepan, add the prawn heads and shells, then fry over medium heat for 3–4 minutes or until golden brown. Add the onion, carrot, celery, leek, fennel, and chilli and cook, stirring frequently, for 10 minutes or until the vegetables are tender. Add the tomato paste and tomato, and cook for another 2–3 minutes, then add the brandy and the remaining olive oil and bring to the boil. Add the star anise, bay leaf, thyme and parsley sprigs and season to taste with salt and pepper, then simmer for 2 hours. Remove from the heat and leave to cool then place in the refrigerator for 2 days. Strain through a muslin-lined sieve placed over a bowl, and leave to sit in the fridge for another day to allow the sediment to settle, then transfer to a glass bottle and seal.

Veal jus

This concentrated stock is incomparable for adding flavour to sauces. It will keep for up to 7 days in the fridge or 3 months in the freezer.

Makes 1 litre

3 kg veal bones
1 tablespoons vegetable oil
1 onion, chopped
½ bulb garlic, cut in half crossways
1 leek, white part only, well-washed and chopped
1 celery stalk, chopped
1 carrots, chopped
2 bay leaves
½ bunch thyme
1 teaspoon white peppercorns
300 ml red wine

Preheat the oven to 160°C. Place the veal bones in a roasting tin and roast until golden brown. Heat the oil in a large saucepan and sauté the onion, garlic, leek, celery, carrot, bay leaves, thyme and peppercorns until the vegetables have softened and the onions are golden brown. Deglaze the pan with the red wine, scraping all the sediment from the bottom of the pan, then add the veal bones and cover with 5 litres of cold water. Bring to the boil, then reduce the heat and simmer for 3 hours, regularly skimming any scum that rises to the surface. Pass the stock through a fine sieve into a clean saucepan, discarding the bones and vegetables, then simmer over medium heat until the jus is reduced to 1 litre. Strain again and leave to cool.

Acknowledgements

There are so many people – chefs, friends and family –
who have helped, inspired and influenced me over the years.

Thanks to: Peter Bartlett, Peter Bracher, Guillaume
Brahimi, Joan Campbell, Genevieve Copeland, Michael De
Laurence, Simon Denton, Sylvain Depuichaffray, Debbie
Donnelley, Sue Fairlie-Cuninghame, Ignazio Fortini, Peter
Harris, Deirdre and Raymond Kirby, the Manfredi family,
Anthony Moran, Carolyn Moran, Jim Moran, Terry and
Debbie Moran, Kirk Pengilly, Alfred Portale, Ruth Ritchie,
Ben Russell, Bruce and Barbara Solomon, Curtis Stone,
Karim Temsamani, Ben Turner, James Valentine, Christopher
Whitehead, Tone Worland, and to all of the staff that have
worked with me over the years.

To all my suppliers: Vic and Anthony Puharich, Barry
and Jamie Macdonald, Simon Johnson, Hugh Wennerbom,
Con Nemitsas, John Sussman.

Many thanks to Gordon Ramsay and Anthony
Bourdain, for taking the time to say a few words about
the book.

To those involved with bringing it together, especially
Julie Gibbs for her professionalism and expertise, the ever-
patient and proficient editor Alison Cowan, and Jay Ryves
for her beautiful design. Thanks also to wonderful stylist
Yael Grinham and, of course, to Geoff Lung: it has been
a pleasure to work with such a gifted photographer. Many
thanks to the following for generously providing props
for the photography: dining table and chair from Thonet;
red fabric from Cloth; Le Creuset cast-iron saucepans and
frying pans from Milners; selected ceramic pieces from Mud
Australia and All Hand Made Gallery.

To the whole ARIA team for their tireless efforts,
especially the awesome pastry chef Andy Honeysett.
A special mention to Simon Sandall, the best chef I've
worked next to, a great mate and partner in the kitchen:
thank you so much for giving me a life outside the kitchen –
I am eternally grateful. Thanks also to all those staff at
ARIA who bore an extra burden while we were working
on the book.

A special and heartfelt thanks to my best mate and
confidant, Michael Moore, and dynamite publicist Sophie
Landa, for looking out for my best interests.

This book simply couldn't have happened without
the Sullivans: Susan, the amazing mother of three (or five,
counting Pete and me), whose ability to pull everything
together through thick and thin continues to astound me;
and Pete – it has been such a privilege over the last fifteen
years to have such a great friend and a partner possessed
with your passion and integrity. I don't know where I
would be without both of you.

And finally to my beautiful wife and life partner, Sarah
Hopkins. Thank you for being so understanding; it's not
easy being married to a chef. For your patience, support
and never-ending love, I thank you from the bottom of
my heart.

Index

LANTERN

Published by the Penguin Group

Penguin Group (Australia)

250 Camberwell Road, Camberwell, Victoria 3124, Australia

(a division of Pearson Australia Group Pty Ltd)

Penguin Group (USA) Inc.

375 Hudson Street, New York, New York 10014, USA

Penguin Group (Canada)

90 Eglinton Avenue East, Suite 700, Toronto ON M4P 2Y3, Canada

(a division of Pearson Penguin Canada Inc.)

Penguin Books Ltd

80 Strand, London WC2R 0RL, England

Penguin Ireland

25 St Stephen's Green, Dublin 2, Ireland

(a division of Penguin Books Ltd)

Penguin Books India Pvt Ltd

11 Community Centre, Panchsheel Park, New Delhi – 110 017, India

Penguin Group (NZ)

Cnr Airborne and Rosedale Roads, Albany, Auckland, New Zealand

(a division of Pearson New Zealand Ltd)

Penguin Books (South Africa) (Pty) Ltd

24 Sturdee Avenue, Rosebank, Johannesburg 2196, South Africa

Penguin Books Ltd, Registered Offices:

80 Strand, London, WC2R 0RL, England

First published by Penguin Group (Australia), a division of Pearson Australia Group Pty Ltd, 2006

1 3 5 7 9 10 8 6 4 2

Text copyright © Matthew Moran 2006

Photographs copyright © Geoff Lung 2006

The moral right of the author has been asserted

Designed by Jay Ryves © Penguin Group (Australia)

Cover photograph by Geoff Lung

Food and props styling by Yael Grinham

Typeset in Glypha and Wilke by Post Pre-press Group, Brisbane, Queensland

Colour reproduction by Splitting Image, Clayton, Victoria

Printed and bound in China by 1010 Printing International Limited

National Library of Australia

Cataloguing-in-Publication data:

Moran, Matt.

Matt Moran.

Includes index.

ISBN-13: 978 1 92098 940 8.

ISBN-10: 1 920989 40 4.

1. Cookery, Australian. I. Lung, Geoff. II. Title.

641.5994

www.penguin.com.au

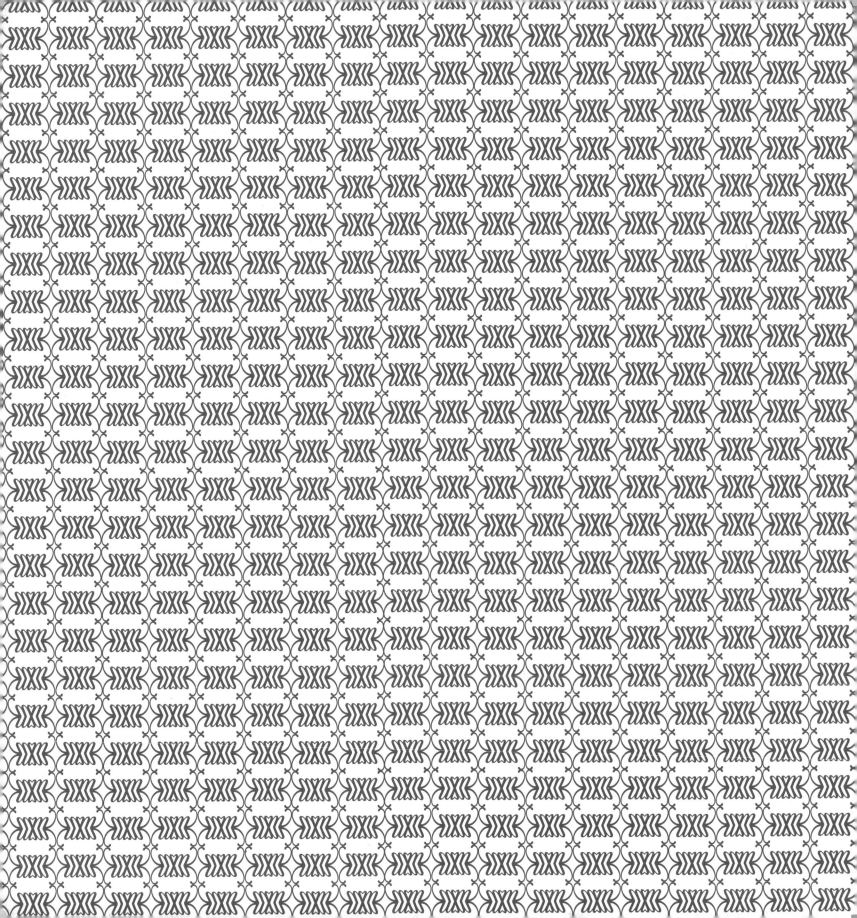